Vision

Book 2

Vision of Sai

Book 2

Rita Bruce

SAMUEL WEISER, INC.

York Beach, Maine

First published in 1995 by
Samuel Weiser, Inc.
Box 612
York Beach, Maine 03910-0612

02 01 00 99 98 97 96 95
11 10 9 8 7 6 5 4 3 2 1

Library of Congress Cataloging-in-Publication Data
Bruce, Rita.
      Vision of Sai / Rita Bruce.
            p.   cm.
      Originally published: A. P., India : Sri Sathya Sai Books and Publications Trust, c1991.
      Includes index.
      1. Sathya Sai Baba, 1926-   I. Title.
BL1175.S385B78   1995
294.5'092--dc20   95-1937
                                                                   CIP

ISBN 0-87728-834-8
EB

Printed in the United States of America

The paper used in this publication meets the minimum requirements of the American National Standard for Permanence of Paper for Printed Library Materials Z39.48-1984.

Dedicated
To the Lotus Feet
of my Beloved

Sri Sathya Sai Baba

TABLE OF CONTENTS

ACKNOWLEDGMENTS

To sing the praises of the Divine Avatar, Sri Sathya Sai Baba, has been a great sadhana and joy for me. With great love and devotion, I offer my thanks to the Divine Lotus Feet of Sai Baba.

Dear friends have helped me shine and polish this book just as Sai shines our soul. While I was in India, Swami gave me permission to publish this book. Sybil Primrose, my Australian friend, read the manuscript and helped enrich the meaning of my words because she understands my writing and the message of Sai Baba. Another dear friend from Norway, Reidun Priddy was visiting Sai Baba when I was working on the book. She graciously read the final manuscript in preparation for publication. How could I be gifted with two equally talented, gentle, kind and loving helpers!

Robert, my husband, loves Sai Baba very much. It is this selfless love that supported, encouraged, inspired and helped in every capacity. He is my spiritual partner. In addition, I thank him for allowing me to share with the world what is normally the private life of a person. Thank you, dear Robert, from my heart.

I also wish to thank my family, for they have touched my life in very special ways. They are the characters that make this story real, each contributing the to the richness of family living.

I ask Sai Baba to bless all these dear people with His Love and I humbly offer them my gratitude.

—Rita Bruce

BOOKS BY AND ABOUT
SRI SATHYA SAI BABA

Available from:

Sathya Sai Book Center of America
305 West First Street
Tustin, Ca 92680

Sri Sathya Sai Baba Books and Publications
Prasanthi Nilayam
Anantapur District
Andhra Pradesh 515134

PERIODICALS

Sanathana Sarathi
Prasanthi Nilayam P.O.
Anantapur District
Andhra Pradesh 515334
India

Sathya Sai Newletters
1800 Easy Garvey Avenue
West Covina, Ca 91791
U.S.A.

INTRODUCTION

I am celebrating my 18th year of knowing Sai Baba, and I can say without any hesitation or reservation, God is on earth in human form, living in India. His name is **SATHYA SAI BABA.** Throughout these years I have experienced and witnessed many miracles, just like in the stories of Jesus, two thousand years ago.

I know, it is utterly incredible. But isn't there a small corner in your mind and heart that wants this to be true? Our planet, our society, and our people are tainted with a disease called selfishness. Overall there is a lack of caring and sharing. There is a lack of concern for mother nature and her people, our brothers and sisters around the world. Who else but God is qualified to correct the severe problems that exist in the world today?

In His Prophetic Discourse, "Why I Incarnate," Sai Baba announced the following in His opening statement:

"For the protection of the virtuous, for the destruction of evil-doers, and for establishing righteousness on a firm footing, I incarnate from age to age. Whenever ashanti, or disharmony, overwhelms the world, the Lord will incarnate in human form to establish the modes of earning prashanti, or peace, and to re-educate the human community in the paths of peace."

In the sixties there was a need to question everything. Sometimes I felt that I may be suddenly robbed of life. The atomic bomb threatened my very existence...... and this triggered deeper thoughts in me. I would think of God and my relationship to Him. I would ask myself: are we living in a world of organized confusion or does God have a plan, a purpose that will eventually win the battle of good over evil? Is our life wasted or can we as individuals contribute to our own soul growth as well as the development of mankind?

Sai Baba through His individual counsel, His teachings and discourses has answered all the questions that I had. The doubts in my mind are erased and replaced with understanding. Where uncertainty prevailed, now certitude reigns.

Can you imagine how peaceful it is to **know** God, His role and ours? To have a moral code, a purpose, and a goal to live for and live by. My agitated mental mind has been put at rest forever. Just imagine how this would change your own life!

We spend millions of dollars trying to buy peace and pleasure. We join golf, tennis, and social clubs, travel, buy bigger and better homes, cars, and boats. We want peace and happiness instead we are unhappy and stressful. We exercise, meditate, swallow natural health foods, anything to quieten our minds and stomachs. The question is: "Are we enjoying life or are we being possessed by it?" Just think that all this expense, time and energy can be forgotten, stopped and substituted with the Divine Love and Teachings of Sai Baba. He says, "I want Peace." Drop the I WANT, and you have Peace.

The greatest attribute that Sai Baba possesses is His ability to transform those that follow His guidance and teachings. He has transformed and changed me into a more peaceful, kinder, caring person. His brilliant light took away the darkness of ignorance, depression, fear of illness and the like. This is one of the reasons I love Him and accounts for the huge numbers that come to see and join Him.

This is why I am so excited. I know the problems I had when I first met Sai Baba. And after 18 years, I know how much He has corrected in me, mentally, physically, emotionally and spiritually. He can fix and heal anything this world offers! He has softened my heart, healed my emotional wounds, and expanded my ability to give and receive Love. All this transformation came from His Divine Love.

Another very helpful experience is being in His Presence. I am able to use His example as a role model and His actions give me a glimpse of my otherwise hidden-self, my God Self. He says, *"I am God, You are God, We are God. The only difference is I Realize it; and you do not."* Therefore the more I see His Loving, Selfless nature, the more I understand my own Divine Nature.

The Love He has is not human. I cannot describe it. But I can share a few thoughts about my own experiences.

Sometimes when I am in His Presence, His aura of love fills my entire being, I lose body awareness, my mind stops and is absorbed by His Beauty. In these precious, timeless moments, I neither want nor need anything but God. I know my goal is to repeat these moments with God into hours, days, months, years till they last for Eternity.

He says, *"My Life is My Message."* He is an example of selfless Love, always giving, asking nothing in return but our love. He says, *"Love must be for its own sake; Love for the sake of fulfilling one's desire is not Love."* He seeks nothing for Himself, always tirelessly working to improve the quality of food, shelter, health care, education, and occupation for the poor and helpless. He tells us, *"LOVE ALL; SERVE ALL."* These are not empty words, but words of fulfillment.

When I first came to see Sai Baba in 1979, there was just a small village at His ashram. Today, it is a town where Sai Baba has built schools to educate boys and girls from Primary school through PH.D. degrees at His University. He has built a General Hospital and a Super Speciality Hospital that is grander than anything seen in the world with the state of the art technology. One section of the Super Speciality Hospital since its inception in November 1991 to February 1994, has performed 2019 heart operations including 1300 open heart. His schools and

INTRODUCTION

hospitals serve mankind FREE OF CHARGE! They are models for the world. Sai Baba says:

> *"There is only one Religion, the Religion of Love.*
> *There is only one Language, the Language of the Heart.*
> *There is only one Race, the Race of Humanity.*
> *There is only one God, and He is Omnipresent."*

He has not come to start a new religion, only to light and reunite those that are already established. He says, *"We are all One, be alike to everyone. Worship the God of your choice. There are many names and forms of God, but He is one. You can be called a son, brother, husband, father, or grandfather and still be the same person with many names. It is the same with God.*

"There is only one sun. It is not different for America, Europe, or India. Just because all the people in the world cannot see the sun at the same time does not mean it does not exist. It is the same with God."

The story of my Spiritual journey begins in my first book, named "VISION OF SAI" by Baba. It covers the first 9 years and there I tell a story of my journey with Sai Baba and how He helped me to mature and spiritually evolve in today's whirlwind culture, using the various roles and relationships in life - devotee wife, devotee mother, and devotee grandmother - stepping stones to lead me along the path becoming a loving servant of God.

Since the women's liberation movement, I had experienced confusion as to the role of wife, mother and/ or career woman. I am married and have four children. The task of managing a household of six was heavy duty and now the emphasis of "Career Woman" was being added to my list of accomplishments. Juggling two jobs in the space of one added stress, exhaustion and unfinished tasks. All this excessive work and pressure because the role of wife and mother was somehow deemed "menial labor".

Today I think, why were the woman's household management skills ignored, or her family therapy techniques overlooked?

It's interesting to note that because of career women, the "Super Mom's" many new occupations have been created. We now have time management courses, more divorce lawyers, day care workers, latch key programs, family counseling etc., etc., which at one time were all assigned to the "housewife"!

Sai's teachings cleared up my confusion about the role of women in society. He helped me to restore honor, dignity and sanity to my full time occupation as wife and mother. "Vision of Sai II" is an extension of the first book and captures the last 9 years with Sai Baba. In 1990, Swami told my husband to retire early. Because of this, we have been blessed to live at Sai Baba's ashram two out of the last three years. Being with Him has stretched and challenged every aspect of our existence. These precious moments I share with you.

Living with Sai God, Master of all teachers, is not easy. Because He excels in cleaning out the impurities within and polishes the "jewel of the heart" till it shines in His light and love. This is my story; the wisdom is His! Woven in the fabric of the text are His Divine threads of wisdom.

He tells us, *"No one hears My name unless I Will it."* This could explain why most of the world is still sleeping, not quite awoken to His identity yet. But He has told us that in the future we will only be able to see a speck of His orange robe because of the crowds that will come. Do not delay, more come every day.

Somehow words seem to fail me, when I try to describe the **Miracle** of Sai Baba. I beg you to read on, not only my book but the many books on His Divine Discourses and devotees' personal experiences. He says *"Come, Investigate and Experience Me."* That is what I hope and dream for you. There is no way I can bring through words the magnamimous Divine Love that Sai Baba gives to us. But I can give you words of hope, and my story of how He has protected, provided, educated, and transformed me. I ask you to "Come, and stay awhile."

Come into His Aura of Love, and Stay All The While.

Note to the reader: All the text that is quoted directly from Sai Baba is in *Italics*.

WRITING

Sai Baba during darshan walked slowly towards my husband, Robert, and paused. Swami told Him to "GO" for an interview. Robert got up and walked towards the veranda. When one member of a family is called it usually includes the rest. As I arose, I remember verbalizing these words but was surprised that I actually spoke them out-loud. "I don't believe it, an interview?"

Only two weeks earlier, I was awakened in the middle of the night hearing my inner voice saying, "You will have **no** interview this trip." The words were clear and distinct. I had no reason to disbelieve especially since the same message was given to me during our 1984 trip to India and proved to be true. Knowing this I couldn't believe my eyes.

As my turn came to walk into the interview room, Sai walked towards me and said, *"I'll see you later."* I moved aside and waited till the ladies cleared the veranda. I

1

started to sit down thinking later meant momentarily. Mataji asked me, "What did Sai Baba tell you?" I replied, "I'll see you later." Mataji said, "Later can mean tomorrow or two years from now," and she ushered me to leave. My heart was in shock and the phrase, "Heart By-Pass" suddenly had a new meaning as I took the most painful walk in my life.

So I quieted myself inside and asked, "What have I done wrong, Swami.... what are you telling me?" I heard His reply. "Two years ago in meditation I told you to write a book, but for the past six months you have stopped." I felt sad that I had let Swami down. Robert was given a private interview and Swami confirmed my inner message by giving Robert the same message. Sai said in a firm tone, *"Your wife should write."* Then with sweetness, He continued, *"I will bless her."*

The question to write or not to write a book had plagued me for several years. It began at a Central Regional Conference during a scheduled hour of silence. I heard my inner voice speak. "I want you to write a book about your experiences with Sai Baba and how His teachings have helped your parents, children, husband and self cope with daily living."

This time I thought my ego had lost its head. "Write a book," I replied. "Swami this is a joke. I can't write. Is this you or me?" I continued to question myself.

Several months after the conference feeling guilty because I had not started to write, I told Swami inside, "There is so much work and activity in this house, how can I write? I need time and quiet."

2

One week later Robert came home from work announcing a great "boon", from his company. He was asked to travel to all their plants in the United States and train the engineers on a system he had designed. He asked if I could travel with him and drive instead of fly. The answer was YES!

I couldn't believe what I was hearing. Three glorious months of traveling! Swami found a way to give me time to write. I could take my typewriter and when Robert went to work, I would stay in the hotel and write all day. This time belonged to Baba. I promised Sai that I would use this time wisely. His Divine Sweetness melted my heart. He gave me so much encouragement to do as He Wills.

We were so happy and the timing was perfect...Divine Timing. The last of our four children, Joan was leaving for her first year of college in two weeks. As she packed for college; I packed for our trip. We took Joan to college and left immediately on our three month journey.

This was the first time we had an empty nest in twenty-five years, no children at home. Just thinking about this stage of our life gave us a sense of freedom and independence. Free to chose our own activities, independent of the family.

Instead of our role as parents, we felt like children, free from our household duties and responsibilities. No chores and no cooking for three months. Parental Liberation! During the week, we both did our duty, Robert trained personnel and I wrote. Then on the weekends we were tourists and played.

3

Sai taught me the true concept of freedom. *"Whenever a man does something for the sake of his personal benefit, it only signifies his desire for that thing. What is involved is not freedom but only the fulfillment of his wish or desire. True freedom emanates from the Heart, irrespective of the place, time, person or thing."*

"What is meant by the heart? It is the Divine principle which is equally present in all persons, at all times, in all places and in all countries. This heart has no form. It is eternal and changeless. Therefore; true freedom consists in recognizing and realizing this Heart or Divine Principle, knowing which,one becomes the knower of everything." Indian Culture and Spirituality p. 135

An added pleasure to this trip was our visits to Sai Centers that were on our route. It's amazing how close we devotees are. Sometimes closer than our immediate family and friends. I would simply call the nearby Center and instantly had the friendship, confidence and trust that usually takes years to build. We could communicate on a personal level and skip the "chit-chat".

The Sai Centers do provide a safety net of knowledge for travelers when distance separates us from our known city or town. The Center devotees can answer any questions we have about their area, spiritual as well as practical. What a gift from God to have this resource at our fingertips not only on a national level but international, as well.

The Sai devotees greeted us with such warmth and hospitality. They may have had the most hectic day but you never knew it. All that was important to them was our comfort and pleasure. Their love is healing in

4

every way.

Sai Baba tells us, *"You must grow in Love, expand that love, practice love, strengthen love, and finally become Love and merge in the Illimitable Love, which is God. All your life, you must be Love, with Love, for Love. That is to say, love expressed through service to those that draw that love from you, and by drawing help to increase it and deepen it."* Sathya Sai Speaks 8, p. 153

This type of service is usually provided by the Center Officers and many times overlooked by center members, because they are not as conscious of the time and effort these "welcome actions" involve. I would like to express for all of us grateful travelers a most loving, THANK YOU.

When I arrived home from the "No Interview Trip," I plunged once again into writing. Sai Baba equipped me with the necessary motivation to do it and a certainty that I should write. I set a daily work schedule and retreated to my office in the house, even though my daughter-in-law lived with me. Since we had a good time being together, it was not easy, but Swami's words still echoed in my ears.... and nothing could prevent me from pleasing Him.

My least favorite subjects in school were spelling and grammar and these were the skills I needed for writing. Sai made me stretch in every conceivable way. I would sit at the typewriter for hours, chugging along. I had heard of people who had the ability to write automatically, knowledge seems to flow through them. How I had hoped that the same would be true for me. I used to sit at the typewriter and say, "Allright, Sai you can begin now." Then I would wait.... and nothing happened until I started doing my own thinking. The only automatic experience I had was that I automatically showed up each day to use the typewriter.

Writing required me to develop new skills. The experience was similar to my primary reading class. Back to the basics. Do you remember our first reading book? "Run Dick, run. Run Jane, run. See Spot, run." I felt inadequate.

I had no practical knowledge on how to write a book nor did I have any college courses, or self-help books. I wrote and re-wrote until it was the way **He** wanted it. I would guess that some chapters took at least 10 re-writes, maybe more.

There were new skills for me to learn. The most difficult was 'logical thinking and a logical sequence'. I wanted my story to be simple, understandable and easy to read. But my thoughts did not appear on the paper in a logical way.

At first the sentences in a given paragraph were so jumbled. The first sentence should be the last and the middle sentence belonged first while the final sentence made absolutely no sense at all. I would cut the sentences apart and reconstruct them like a jig-saw puzzle. The entire floor of my office was covered with scraps of paper. I'll never forget how threatened I felt when Robert came home with a computer. After months of writing, I had finally developed a style of editing my material. I would cut and tape the sentences and paragraphs together that I wanted to use. This method was beginning to feel familiar, and I thought I was finally making some progress. Now he was asking me to learn a completely new process. I was upset. I actually resented having to start over again, but I tried.

Robert was teaching me to use a computer program called "Word Star". It seemed foreign and difficult until, one night when we were working together, Robert told me that I was feeling "threatened" by this machine and my mind was creating barriers that prevented me from attaining this new skill. He was right. Once I accepted my negative attitude and realized I was creating my own problem, the learning process became easier. If I had quit and not changed my attitude, I would have missed using the greatest invention for writing and editing since the printing press.

My writing skill did improve with practice and seeing this progress inspired me to continue. I also received encouragement from Sai Baba through the Sanathana Sarathi journal. Several articles that I wrote were published during this phase of my writing and they always appeared when I was very disappointed and felt hopeless.

Sai Baba knew that it would take enormous effort for me to accomplish the task of writing a book. His corrective action of turning me away from the interview room was exactly the strong medicine I needed to overcome my insecurity about writing. The gift He gave to me that day was the desire to succeed. I was **determined** not to return empty-handed and I had the strongest desire to see Swami and regain His Grace. This

7

kept my effort intense.

Believe me, when you have failed Swami and know He loves us so much you want to correct your behavior quickly and again hear His voice say, *"Very Very Happy."*

The Master of Teachers again taught me that I can accomplish anything with His love and guidance, as long as I apply the necessary effort. I deeply understand and know that He will shape me into His Loving image as long as I continue to showup. I no longer need Faith, because I **know** that Sai Baba can remove any problematic situation, any inherited karmic characteristic, or any animalistic behavior within my scope of reality and beyond. He has enhanced my self-confidence and ensured and secured a stronger foundation in my personality, so the liability of weakness, rot or decay is cleaned away.

When our most vivid experiences pass from the reality of the moment into memory, the development of greater character is more important than the struggle to attain. All of life is truly He; no problem, if we can remove the "me!"

*"The highly talented persons in different walks of life have not acquired their skills from some where outside. All these are but manifestations of their own innate potentialities. It is sheer ignorance to think that any person can be developed by some other person. Everything is in you alone. All that you do by way of **your effort** is to manifest or give an outer expression to what is already inherent in you.* Indian Culture and Spirituality, p. 135

8

It was March, about 13 months since we departed from Prasanthi Nilayam, the writing was progressing and I needed a break. Robert and I took a trip to the Lake of the Ozarks and decided to look at some condominiums. For years we had been taking the family camping there. We got lost, and found a condominium project that had just come out of bankruptcy and opened that morning. It was purchased by an architect/builder who was ready to develop the remaining property.

We were surprised when we heard that the project had been built by our favorite builder on the Lake. When we entered the condominiums, it was exactly what we had dreamed of but knew we could never afford. This builder was definitely beyond our price range. Can you imagine our shock and surprise when we were quoted a price $35,000 below the market value?

A star from heaven fell right into our lap. Fifteen minutes later we owned a beautiful condominium with a magnificent view of the lake. We named it Prasanthi, our abode of Peace. Many times that year, I went to the lake, alone with Sai to write.

WHAT IS FREEDOM?

How glittering and quivering is the water drop on the lotus leaf!

So is man's life in this transient world; life is filled with strife, disease and delusion.

Sorrow and suffering reign supreme in this sordid world.

Therefore, oh foolish mind! Take refuge in the name of the Lord.

DIVINE DISCOURSE

*D*ear Students, people in general cannot understand what spirituality and individual freedom are. Spirituality does not mean living in solitude, far away from society. True spirituality consists of sowing the seeds of love in the hearts of all people and facilitating the blossoming of peace and divine love among all mankind. If you inquire deeply into the nature of the Divine Principle, there are not two things like spirituality and individual freedom.

If one is allowed to express one's feelings and thoughts from a public platform without any hindrance, it is said to be individual freedom. But the truth is that no one has absolute freedom in this universe. The word "freedom" has been used frequently in the political field. What is freedom? To get rid of foreign rule and to establish the rule

11

of the natives of the nation was considered to be freedom before India got her political independence. But that was neither individual freedom nor fundamental freedom. It was only a replacement of foreign rule by indigenous rule, with little or no change in the aspect of freedom as such. After the departure of the foreigners, we thought that the natives acquired freedom. But in what aspect did we get freedom? What is the use of simply repeating, "freedom, freedom." It is only when we have achieved unity that we can claim to have attained freedom. Without achieving unity, if we talk of freedom, it is merely the freedom of words but not of individuals. True freedom springs forth from the level of the Heart.

What is meant by the "Heart?" Not the physical heart full of flesh and blood. The real Heart is that which has no connection with any particular place, time, individual or country. It is the Divine Principle which is equally present in all persons at all times, in all places and in all countries. This Heart has no form. What we consider as the heart inside the human body comes in the middle and goes in the middle. But what we call "Heart" in the spiritual parlance knows no coming or going; it is eternal and changeless. Therefore, true freedom consists in recognizing and realizing this Heart or Divine Principle - knowing which one is the Knower of everything.

As in the microcosm, so in the macrocosm. Microcosm refers to the individual and macrocosm to the aggregate or sum total. One who knows the Self knows all. Today people try to know everything about the world; they feel proud that they know everything. But they forget that they do not know themselves. Mention is made in one of the Upanishads of a *great sage by the name Uddalaka who sent his son Svetaketu to a guru to be educated. Svetaketu took twelve years to acquire proficiency in all the branches of learning. Puffed up with pride, he returned to his father and told him about his profound scholarship. Then the father questioned him, "Oh my son, do you know that by knowing That, you would know everything?" The son was baffled by this question which gave a shattering blow to his pride of learning. Of all the kinds of pride, the pride of learning is the worst. By putting that question to his son, it made sage Uddalaka recognize the superiority of Self-knowledge, or Atma Jnanam, as compared to Loka Jnanam, or secular knowledge.*

When you ask someone, "Who are you?" and if they reply, "I don't know who I am," what do you think of them? You consider them to be mad. Similarly, if you try to know about everything else without knowing who you are, are you any better than that mad person? Therefore, you should try to know who you are. You may say, "I am called Ramaiah." But Ramaiah is the name given to your body. What is that "I" in your reply who is separate from Ramaiah? You should understand the nature of "I"; That "I" is nothing other than the Heart. That "I" is the Atma or Self. That "I" is Brahman or the Supreme Reality. This Heart is all-pervasive, omnipresent.

Consider this illustration: A painter has painted a beautiful picture of a dancing girl on a sheet of paper. The picture shows her body and limbs with several bends and curves, ups and downs in the process of dancing. In another painting, there are high mountains and low valleys. But if you feel the paper by touching it, you will not find any ups and downs or elevations and depressions in either painting. So also, in the phenomenal world, you find many differences like ups and downs, good and bad, sins and virtues, truth and untruth, pain and pleasure, etc. But at the level of the Heart, you will not find these dualities or pairs of opposites.

Let us consider another example. There is a silver tumbler. It has a name and a form. If you remove or ignore the name and form, what remains? Only silver; it was silver before becoming a tumbler. When it has the form of a tumbler, it remains silver. If the tumbler is destroyed and made into a round mass, it will continue to be silver. So it is nothing but silver in the beginning, the middle and the end. The name and form of the tumbler was there only in the middle, but not in the beginning or at the end. That which does not exist in the beginning and the end, but exists only in the middle is considered to be nonexistent, even in the middle. Its apparent existence in the middle is only a myth or illusion. That is why the phenomenal world is called mithyajagath, the illusory universe.

Existence is one. When there is no second, how can the question of freedom or bondage arise? So these concepts of freedom and bondage are the concoctions of your own mind. For example, we give attention and value to the moon only when there is no sun. Why do we give value to the moon when there is no sun? The moon has no effulgence of its own. It shines because of the reflection of the sun's rays. Similarly, when we do not see the sun of Self; we give value to the moon of the mind. The Vedas have revealed that the mind is a reflection of the moon. Therefore, we cherish the mind and nourish it by devoting more time and attention to

14

it, but we neglect Atma vichara or Self-inquiry. It is only when you have the mind, that you see all differences as spiritual or secular, sacred or mundane, freedom or bondage, man or woman, prakriti or Paratatwam (nature or Absolute Reality). All dualities are certainly creations of the mind.

I wish to clarify some points relating to the debate that took place here on the subject of "Freedom and Bondage." Suppose there is a man suffering from dire poverty; he is very hungry. Even in spite of begging, no one gives him food. Then he feels that he has the freedom to resort to stealing in order to appease his hunger. Although he may rationalize thus, because of his selfishness, his conscience does not approve of his stealing. So how can it be called freedom when his conscience disapproves? It may, at best, be called freedom with bondage. When does one have real freedom? Only when the mind is destroyed. When you use the words swabhava and swechcha, you have to understand their true meaning. Swa means Self or Atma. Hence, swabhava means the nature of Atma. Likewise, swa+ichcha equals swechcha which means the volitions or power of the Atma. Strictly speaking, it should be understood as volition which is in line with the Atma, since Atma, per se, has no volition. In the light of these meanings, it is incorrect to use the terms swabhava and swechcha in connection with matters relating to the activities of the body, senses, mind and intellect.

It should be recognized that man's life is regulated by the laws of nature on the one hand, and by the man-made regulations on the other. Such being the case, there is no validity in thinking that one has freedom to act as they like.

15

It is only God who may be said to have freedom. Even this is a relative truth, because in absolute terms, existence is only one; hence, the word "freedom" is out of place in this context.

People talk glibly about surrender. Some persons complain, "I have completely surrendered myself to Swami, but there is no end to my problems, hardships, suffering and sorrow." In my view, this is not surrender at all. True surrender never cognizes the presence or absence of sorrow, suffering, misery and the like. There are some others who say, "When I sit in meditation, I sometimes go into samadhi." But what is samadhi? In books written by worldy people with mundane views, one may find various descriptions of samadhi. While in meditation, a person may lose body-consciousness. But this cannot correctly be called samadhi. It may be a symptom of weakness, fits, hysteria or emotion, but never a sign of samadhi. In that state, one does not see or experience duality. Samadhi equals sama plus dhi, which essentially means equalmindedness. In that condition, there will be no trace of such differences like pleasure and pain, gain and loss, virtue and sin or prakriti and Paramatma - nature and God. This alone is the evidence of equalmindedness. This truly is swabhava, nature of the Self. In contrast, if a person aspires for something and pursues various paths to achieve it, you may take it as an indication of their mental aberrations.

As long as the mind is there, no one can claim to be enjoying freedom. In the worldly parlance, one may say, "I have money. I am giving it to someone. This is my free will, etc." But truly speaking, this is neither freedom nor free will. The mind is a mixture of three qualities or gunas:

16

sathwic (pure, calm, unruffled), rajasic (overly active, craving adventure) and tamasic (dull, ignorant, lazy). One or more of these three may become dominant at a given time in any person. In the present instance, the mind of the man who is giving some money to another person is motivated by the sathwic guna, to give something in charity to a needy person. Hence, when a man acts under the influence of the gunas, how can he claim to have freedom of will? It is therefore impossible for anybody, who is part of creation, to have freedom.

Justice Khastagir said that a person has freedom to conduct physical exercise by waving a stick in the compound of his home. But he has no freedom to do so in a public place, because it is against governmental regulations, and he is liable to be arrested by the police. Strictly speaking, when a man does exercise by waving a stick on the premises of his residence, that which is involved is not freedom but only the fulfillment of his desire. Whenever a man does something for the sake of his personal benefit, it signifies his desire for that thing. True freedom emanates only from the Heart irrespective of the place, time, person or thing.

Highly talented people, in different walks of life, have not acquired their skills from somewhere outside. All skills are manifestations of their own innate potentialities. It is sheer ignorance to think that any person can be developed by some other person. Everything is in you already. All that you do by way of your effort is to manifest or give an outer expression to what is already inherent within you. So even in the spiritual field, all the sadhana (spiritual activity) that you need to do is to remove the obstruction, namely, the

17

ignorance that is preventing the manifestation of the Divinity already present in you. Krishna too taught this truth to Arjuna as follows:

"Arjuna, you did not know the art and science of archery when you were born. You are under the impression that Drona instructed you, and therefore, you acquired the skills of warfare from somewhere outside. It is not correct to think that Drona taught you and that you learned these skills afresh. All that Drona did was to facilitate the manifestation of what was already in you." Remember that any teacher or great person endowed with extraordinary powers cannot bring out what is not already inside you. Good luck or bad luck, bliss or misery - all these are in you.

Suppose you are digging a well. On reaching the depth of, say, 100 feet, you strike a good spring with a copious supply of water. Now, have you created the water or brought it from somewhere? No, the water was there all the while; it came to view because the earth that was covering it was removed. So too, there is Divinity ever present in you, but you have forgotten it. Why did you forget? Because of your wrong identifcation with the body.

As long as there is mind, man cannot escape from various kinds of thoughts. These indicate the freedom of the mind, but not freedom of the person. Sampath (Vice Chancellor of the Sri Sathya Sai Institute of Higher Learning) has told you that a student has the freedom to question the teacher and obtain answers. But this does not come under freedom; it comes under duty. The duty of a student is to abide by the regulations of the educational system which provides for asking questions and obtaining answers. You should understand the difference between freedom and duty. Duty may be considered under three categories: sambandham meaning relationship, nirbandham meaning compulsion and kartavyam meaning obligation. Here are examples of the differences between these three:

You want to give a tea party for your friends on a Sunday evening. You invite your friends in advance. But at 4:00 PM on Sunday you develop a high temperature. So you inform all the invitees that the tea party is postponed. In this situation, you may or may not have the tea party, as you wish. But this is not freedom; it is sambandham, relationship - something voluntary and optional.

About nirbandham, you are in the office, suddenly you are attacked by a high fever. On that very day, your boss is coming to inspect your office. So you cannot go on leave of absence. Therefore, you run to the doctor - take an injection and some tablets for your illness - and remain in your office compulsorily, in spite of your suffering from the fever. This is a case of nirbandham or compulsion.

Third is kartavyam. Due to some reasons there arises a quarrel between you and your wife... She goes away into the bedroom and lies down, weeping. She does not attend to the cooking. You are sitting in the drawing room. You are extremely angry on two accounts: First, for the reason which led to your quarrel and second, because your wife has not cooked food and you are very hungry. So due to the combination of both anger and hunger, you are very restless. Just then a good friend comes to visit. You greet him with a smile saying, "Hello, hello" and after offering him a seat, you go inside and tell your wife in a hushed voice but with an angry tone, "Our friend has come; prepare coffee." You show an angry face to your wife but a happy countenance to your friend. You don't want your friend to know that you are angry with your wife, nor do you want your wife to know that you are jolly with your friend. You are thus obliged to adjust your behavior to suit different persons and situations in conformity with the social norms and etiquette. This is called kartavyam or obligation.

Nowadays, people in general have given the go-by to all three - sambandham, nirbandham and kartavyam - relationship, compulsion and obligation. Hence there is dharmaglani - an all-around decline of righteousness in modern society. It should be noted that there is no freedom for man in acting according to relationship, compulsion and obligation as illustrated above. There is freedom only at the level of the Atma or Self.

Engage yourself in any activity, but always keep in view your true nature as the Self or Atma. If you do so, you will surely enjoy real freedom. There are not two kinds of freedom, individual and spiritual. Spirituality alone is freedom. Freedom alone is spirituality. It is not possible for these two to exist separately. There is only one entity which has assumed different names and forms. Just as the same milk assumes the different names and forms like: curd, yogurt, buttermilk, cream, butter and more. Similiarly, saalokyam, saameepyam, saaroopyam and saayujyam are different names for the same spiritual experience. These four, however, are progressive steps in the process of God-realization. Saalokyam means always thinking of God and living in the spiritual world or God's world, so to say, instead of the material world. Saameepyam indicates moving closer to Swami or God. Saaroopyam means becoming one with Swami. Saayujyam is the final stage of becoming Swami Himself, therefore, complete merger without any trace of duality.

If anyone in this phenomenal world says he has freedom, we can call it only "crazy freedom." It may also be called freedom of the ego, and freedom of infatuation or attachment. It is foolish on your part to think you have the freedom to scold or strike your wife or children. If you want to enhance your freedom by suppressing the freedom of others, it is only utter selfishness. True freedom lies in not interfering with the freedom of others. What you find in this world is a hierarchy of controls, the one at a higher level controlling the one at a lower level. This results in a lack of freedom for all except perhaps for the one person at the top of the hierarchy. But strictly speaking, even that one person occupying the topmost rung of the hierarchical ladder cannot be said to have freedom, because the question of freedom does not arise when there is only one without a second. What we call individual freedom and fundamental rights may serve the purpose of enabling us to carry on our mundane affairs. But in the absolute sense, there is no true freedom involved in these matters.

From the above discussion, we arrive at the conclusion that - from whatever angle we may consider the matter - there is no freedom for mankind, and that there can be no freedom for mankind. In fact, man does not know what true freedom means. One who has freedom does not take birth in this world. One who enters the world with a body cannot have freedom. Take the example of an animal tied to a peg with a ten foot length of rope to illustrate that the animal has a limited freedom within a radius of ten feet. But how can you speak of its freedom when the animal is tied and it cannot go beyond ten feet? **Anything that is bound by any limitation whatsoever, cannot and should not be said to have freedom.** This only shows that we are in the habit of using words without knowing their correct meaning.

If you understand the true meaning of Heart, you will recognize that it is beyond all limitations. The same Heart that is within you is also within all others including those who are hated by you or who hate you. You may wonder - if all have the same Heart - why should their thoughts, attitudes and actions be different? Students, remember that all these differences are created by the mind and they have nothing to do with the Heart. This is not the physical heart but the spiritual Heart which is omnipresent. It has no form, but it is the substratum for all forms. It can be compared to sugar which is the common basis for all kinds of sweets enjoyed by different people.

All the differences you find in the world are only reflections of your mind. Whether you love or hate someone, ridicule or praise them, it is only your reflection. If you give up these reactions and reflections - which appear in the phenomenal world and get hold of the Heart, which is Reality then all these differences in thoughts, feelings and actions will disappear. God does not have thoughts and feelings of any kind. But He appears to respond suitably according to the thoughts, feelings, attitudes and actions of the devotees. God has no likes or dislikes; nor is He angry

22

with some and pleased with others. He does not have moods that change from time-to-time in respect to the same person or different people, as many of you imagine. Of course, as a result of putting on a body, the Avatars appear to have such reactions and reflections, but it is only to set an example for others and to help them reform themselves, so they may make the needed progress in their spiritual journey. God does not differentiate or discriminate between high caste or low caste, between the young or the old, between men or women, between people of one country or another, etc., etc. These are all mundane differences pertaining to the world, but they have nothing to do with Divinity.

It is only narrow - mindedness to think that Rama was born into a Kshatriya family, Krishna into the Yadava or cowherd family, or Sai Baba into Raju - Kshatriya family and so on. God will never have such differences. If one correctly understands the nature of the Divine Principle of the Atma, there will be no cause for such petty, narrow-minded differences and discriminations.

Living in this vast universe, you must develop broad thoughts and feelings to understand the nature of the infinite Atma. Spirituality should not be approached from a narrow standpoint. Doing worship, devotional singing, meditation and the like are considered by many as signs of spirituality. But all these are mental aberrations that serve to give only mental satisfaction to the practitioners. You praise God, saying "Lord, you are my mother, my father, my friend" and so on. But why all this mumbo-jumbo and gibberish? Why not simply say, "You are I. I am You" and be done with it? In this connection, it is not correct to say,

23

"You and I are one", because you and I are we, but never one. It is better to say, "We and we are one," because I am in you and you are in me. Therefore, when we come together, we become one. However in the statement, "We and we are one" there is duality because the "we" consists of the physical body and the Divine Principle of the Atma. If you understand the nature of these two aspects of your personality, you will never think of the relationship between yourself and God like mother, father, friend etc. You are both one, although you may appear as two. Here is a concrete illustration for this. The mike in front of me appears as two but functions as one in the process of amplifying my voice to make it audible. Similarly, you should visualize and realize the unity of the body and the Atma. This is the one sadhana (spiritual discipline) you should practice.

Students, spirituality means merger with God. You are not different from God. You are God; God is you. If you are firmly established in this faith, you need not undertake any other sadhana or spiritual practice. Of course, some people repeat parrot - like, "I and You are one," but they do not live up to it. Here is a small story to illustrate this: A guru gave the mantra Sivo-ham to one of his disciples and told him that the mantra means, "I am Siva." As the disciple was uttering, "Sivo-ham, Sivo-ham," a friend of his came and asked him about the meaning of the mantra. On being told the meaning, the friend questioned him, "If you are Siva, how is Parvati related to you?" The immediate response of the disciple was, "May God forgive my offence! Goddess Parvati is far superior to me and deserves my adoration and worship." The point to be noted here is that if the

24

disciple had real faith and conviction in the mantra Sivoham, which implies that there is only one God - who appears to have assumed all the names and forms of all gods and goddesses, as well as all beings in the universe - then the correct answer to his friend's question would have been, "I am Parvati too."

Instead, this wrong reply was due to his belief in the traditional husband-wife relationship that Parvati was Siva's consort. Therefore, these kinds of complications will arise if you think of God in terms of such worldy, physical relationships like mother, father, etc. Instead of that, you should have unshakeable faith in the unity of Godhead and assert, "I am You, You are I - we are not two, but one." This is the true freedom inherent in you. In this context, you should understand the correct meaning of the terms swadharma and paradharma used in the Gita. The meaning of Swadharma is Atma-dharma, and not the dharma or duties enjoined on the different castes like Brahmanadharma, Kshatriya-dharma and so on. Likewise, paradharma means dehadharma or dharma pertaining to the body. It is in this sense that you should understand the declaration in the Gita, "par-adharmo bhayavahah," which, in effect, means that if you follow the deha-dharma or the dharma of the physical body, fear will be your lot in life. On the other hand, if you follow the Atma-dharma, you will have no fear. If you understand the real meaning of the verses and words in the Gita and if you mold your lives accordingly, you will have no fear of slander, ridicule, sorrow or suffering.

Students, you may or may not believe me when I say, "I do not know what sorrow is, what worry is, or what *hardship means." Some may praise and worship me. Others may criticize and vilify me. It is their will and pleasure in either case. I am not at all bothered. My attitude toward others abusing me is, if they abuse or scold me aloud, I say, 'Gone with the wind.' If they abuse me silently within themselves, I say, 'It hurts only them, for it does not reach me.' In either case, why should I be worried at all? Therefore, if you are established in truth, you will never be affected by praise or blame, by joy or sorrow. People come to me and complain about the bereavements in their family or some suffering and pain etc. I respond to them by saying 'Chaala santosham,' which means, "Very happy." You should note that this kind of happiness remains the same under all circumstances, because it is based on the Atmatatwa which means, "Everything is Atma." However, sometimes I pretend to be angry with the students, because of their wrong behavior. But it is only outward anger; it does not come from inside. I may not speak to some persons for months. That is the medicine to cure them of their disease of misbehavior and to correct them. What right has anybody to ask why Swami is not talking to them?*

A small example of this: Four patients go to a doctor. They have all come with the same complaint of stomach ache. The doctor examines them one after the other. He gives one of them the advice to have hot water fomentation. For the second patient, he gives a mixture of mag sulph and soda bicarb and tells him that he will be relieved of his stomach ache which is due to gas trouble. For the third person, he gives some tablets. But he wants the fourth person to undergo an operation immediately because his stomach pain is due to appendicitis. Similarly, I give

26

different treatments to different people based on their needs and for their own good. I don't even look at some people. I don't speak to some. I avoid or pass by others, although they try to attract my attention. These are all my prescriptions for their respective diseases. Why do I administer such medicines or treatments? I have principles; my words are very precious. Even if you don't give value to my words; I attach great importance and value to them. If somebody does not heed my words, I don't like to waste them by speaking to him. Hence, in order to save the value of my words, I stop talking to such persons. Instead of complaining that Swami does not talk to you, why don't you blame yourself for not acting according to Swami's instructions? This is not one-way traffic; it is a matter of give and take. If Swami's orders are implicitly obeyed by you, His grace is showered on you automatically. You need not specially pray for His grace. First of all, attach value to your own words. Remember the wise saying, "Truth is the life of a word; a battalion of brave soldiers is the life of a fort; modesty is the life of a woman; and signature is the life of a promissory note."

All cannot understand the nature of Divinity. God is never elated or depressed. Even if the whole world blames and reviles me, I will not be depressed. Even if the entire world extols me, I will not be elated. This is because I am established in Truth. There will be no room for any worry or anxiety if you are firmly established in Heart, Atma or Truth - all of which mean the same. Try to understand the Divinity of Swami who is the changeless support of all that changes. Thus sanctify and justify your stay here.

Indian Culture and Spirituality
Summer Course 1990

27

HOMECOMING

The phone rang and I heard Donna saying, "Hi mom." It always amazed me that she would call after months of absence and speak as if nothing transpired in between our last conversation. "Mom," she continued, "I've got some news for you. You're going to be a grandmother. I'm six months pregnant." Her tone was one of happiness, she seemed pleased. But Donna was not married and her joy met the maturity of a parent whose child was having a child out-of-wedlock. I loved being a grandparent but hearing the news this time was different. All I could think of was the difficult life of a single parent, and a child with no father.

I tried not to dump my fear for her future on her happy feelings. I inquired about the father and was told that it was her boyfriend John that she had been supporting for the past three years. He was the son of an alcoholic mother. As well as the son of an alcoholic child-

29

abusing father.

John had a very poor childhood and it was affecting his manhood. He drank heavily and had no job. I heaved a sigh and silently called SAI. 'What's next,' I thought? 'What a mess.'

The story about Donna's drug and alcohol habit is in my first book, Vision of Sai.

Her child was born on July 11, 1987. Donna called from the hospital while she was in labor. She was crying in pain and was calling for my help. I tried to calm and explain the process of child delivery to her. She had had no childbirth preparation or training. Her hysteria from the pain was intensified by the fear of the unknown. As I closed our conversation I knew it was beneficial for me to give her a sense of self-control by taking some positive action to help relieve her agony.

"Donna, do you have a light by your bed that you can press to call the nurse?" She looked and said, "Yes." "Press it, Donna," I said, "and explain to the nurse what pain you are feeling. She will help you. Everything will be all right, you're becoming a mother and what's happening is normal. You're OK. I'll pray to Baba. I'll be here; if you need me." She lived about 900 miles from us in Minnesota.

It was about midnight. I hung up the phone and inwardly yelled for Swami. "Oh Baba," I cried, "this child does not understand what is happening to her. She can't cope, Lord. I feel so helpless. Take her pain away, please Baba, come to her aid." How I begged for His mercy! I went back to bed and laid awake praying for her.

Sai says, *"The tiniest suffering in you causes the same suffering here also."* Sathya Sai Speaks 4, p. 35

One hour later, the phone rang and I jumped up to get it. Oh God, I thought, here we go again. Never did I expect to be greeted with the words, "You're a grandma; it's a girl" !

I said, "You've had the baby already? It's only been an hour!" This is unusual because the first child normally takes longer to deliver. Donna re-affirmed to her disbelieving mother and said, "Mom, it's a girl and I had no more pain after I talked with you." My heart overflowed, with a flood of gratitude to Sai Baba. "No more pain, I asked?" She responded, "No more pain."

I prayed for a miracle but why was I so awed by the fulfillment of my petition? It's not that I disbelieve in God's wonderful grace, but I guess the reason comes from often having prayers answered in a different time and manner than expected. It's nice, Lord, to experience your instant reply. Many times my prayers seem to be unanswered but they are simply put on God's repair list and who knows how, when, or even what will happen. It's so refreshing to find the painful plight of another removed so quickly.

In August, Donna called and asked, "MOM, I want to come home and bring John." "Donna," I said, "I'm really not interested." "But mom," she continued, "He may be your new son-in-law and I think its time you met. You tell us to forgive. Don't you think you should do the same with John?"

Donna was referring to an incident that had happened a year ago when John had abused my daughter. She was asking a lot from us. She certainly knew how to hit the right button, Baba must be coaching her! Teach by example is the basis of Sai's teachings, and the word forgiveness quickly flashed spiritual teachings into my mind...... *"Love is giving and forgiving,"* says Sai. To err is Human, to forgive, Divine, etc.

I told her I would discuss her request with her dad and asked her to call back in two days. She didn't have a phone where she was staying.

Sai says, *"Do not regard anything as bad. If a person has done evil to you and you take it as evil and retaliate, then you also have become bad. But, by remaining good and not regarding others as evil, you gain the right to reform them. Bad actions should be met with good deeds and good viewpoint, and the evil will be changed."* Conversations, p. 102

It was this teaching that influenced us. We both wanted to help them and hoped that if we gave them a new start, perhaps it would change their life. We showered them with Sai's Love.

When she called, we told her to come home with John. Within a few days they arrived in St. Louis. It was late at night and we decided to meet them instead of giving instructions. This way there was no chance of them getting lost. They were driving a rusted out old jalopy. Swami must have held it together. It was dark and Donna looked so thin and the baby only weeks old. My heart melted. They called her Tara Marie. Tara means "light".

Robert and I loved little Tara almost immediately. There seems to be a very strong bond between us.

It was good to have Donna home again. Robert and I consciously decided to give John our love and understanding. To remove all our pre-conceived thoughts and concepts that had formed from the past stories we had heard from Donna. We started our relationship anew, hoping to give them no negativity or criticism from past actions. This was their chance and we were not going to put any negativity in their path. Our attitudes were adjusted, our hearts were open and ready to receive the Lord's Love and share it with them.

"Spread joy at all times. Do not pour into others' ears your tales of woe and worry; carry a smile on your face so that every one who sees you can catch the exhilaration. When you tell others of your success, your purpose is to create envy in them. You must not only love others, but you must be so good that others too may love you. Try to console, encourage, strengthen, and enlighten those who are miserable, downhearted, weaker, ill-informed. Get yourselves equipped for this role." Sathya Sai Speaks 4, p. 274

They wanted to move to St. Louis and begin a new life. Of course, we agreed. I was never more hopeful.

Sai Baba was so good. Every detail was taken care of by Swami. They moved to Lake Ozark, it is a small town like the one they came from in Minnesota, and they felt more comfortable there than in a big city. Since our condo was also there we would have many opportunities to see them. It was ideal.

They each got good jobs, one worked in the day and the other worked in the evening. No baby-sitter was needed. We provided the household goods and furniture, mostly from family and garage sales. We found a nice condominium, gave them a car and provided an income till they received their wages. The obvious obstacles were all removed. Success was now in their hands.

It lasted three months then John walked out on Donna. He had never committed to marriage and had found himself another partner. Most of their income he spent on alcohol.

We told Donna that if she would leave him permanently; we would continue to help her. We had talked with her brother and sisters and they were all wanting to help her start a new life. She was to call us in a day or two but...... she never called.

Upon investigation the police found an empty condo. The furniture was gone and so was Donna. We had no idea where she and the baby were, but we did know: Donna could not decide to leave John. The possibility of his return to her life some day was evident.

Sai says, *"Today the world is riddled with fear. Whether at home, or out in the street, or while traveling in a train, bus or plane, people are haunted by fear. The root cause for this ubiquitous fear is the absence of pure and sacred thoughts in the minds of men. The whole world appears like a maze filled with fear at every turn."* Indian Culture and Spiritually p. 71

I asked myself, "Why is my child so blind to the love we want to give her? Why does she choose to live with a person who abuses her? Is there no self-love or self-esteem present in her suffering soul? Oh, how I hate to see her pain. Why is she so blind to the love and help we want to give her? Why, Swami can't Donna lean on us till she finds her own strength?

When she gets afraid, she runs. How I worried about their well-being! She had so little money. Where did they sleep? Did they eat? Who was there to hold them in their arms? Oh, Baba, you are the one who provides for everything. How limited we felt. When the control was removed from our hands and there was nothing we could do, we surrendered. In these extreme cases of helplessness God's power becomes self-evident.

We realized that as long as she ran into the arms of a man who was abusing her and who was sick with the disease of alcohol, there was nothing that we could do to help her. We had tried. This was the second time we set Donna up in a furnished home. The same thing happened again. The change must come from within her... there is nothing we can do but cling to Swami.

There is a parallel here, I thought. Many times Baba tells us that we do not come to Him to receive what He has to give. Instead we come to fulfill our habits and desires. We too are blind to the reality of the Love He wishes to bestow on us, and He too is hand-cuffed because He must wait for us to decide and choose to change. Through motherhood Swami has taught me so much about God and His relationship with us. Being a parent is most difficult but it also has given me compassion and insight. It softened my heart.

Our hopes for Donna were crushed. I asked, "Are our children safe? Where are they resting their heads tonight?" The baby is so young, only a few months. Now there were two to worry about, Donna and little Tara who stole our hearts. We did not know where they were. I felt so empty.

When the night grows chill, you draw the rug tighter around you, is it not? So too when grief assails you, draw the warmth of the name of the Lord closer round your mind. Sathya Sai Speaks 4, p. 36

MANUSCRIPT

It was time for our trip to India to see Sai Baba and I had a completed manuscript! This year, I had concentrated most of my energy on writing. I had to discipline myself daily, and realized this little exercise was really one of the reasons why Swami had got me involved with writing. It really makes no difference what we do for Swami; it's the lessons we learn from the action that builds the character that we need to achieve our spiritual goals.

I was extremely happy because my effort had produced a manuscript. I wanted so much to present it to Swami. I felt like a child who had been disobedient, corrected and disciplined by its parent and now was returning home, reformed and looking for approval from the Divine Father.

Hidden within the script of this thinking was an expectation, that my parent Lord Sai Baba would

37

welcome me with open arms. I did not want to think about of the opposite happening even though I knew this was a possibility. I was only interested in His acceptance and recognition. All I wanted Him to say was, "You did good!"

Even though I know that He wants me to assume the role of an adult, sometimes I assume the role of a child in my relationship to Sai Baba. It's so easy to be childish because of the nature of God and His role as our Divine Parents. He protects, guides, and provides. He tells us to depend on Him for everything. Surrender to Him.

But depending on our Divine Parent is different from surrendering: I can depend on Swami for all my needs, like a child depends on his parents, but surrender must be defined as, **He determines my needs.**

Sai Baba is working with all of us, teaching each one to become adult, spiritually adult. The goal of every earthly parent is to teach their children to become self-sufficient. The goal of every child is to become adult. When children think they are mature and want the responsibility for making their own decisions, they are often unaware that hidden within that script is also the responsibility for the consequences of their actions. The same is true concerning my relationship with Sai Baba. Even though I understand the relationship, my feelings are still those of a child, wanting His acceptance unconditionally.

We arrived at His ashram on the 23rd of December, tired but anxious to get to our room, clean it, and relax before afternoon darshan. We are "allottees." This means the accommodation office uses our room for guests who visit Sai Baba throughout the year but when we arrive we are given preference, and whoever is using our room is asked to vacate.

The ladies in our room didn't want to move until later in the day. I could understand their resistance especially if they needed to go to the sheds or change from one building to another. However these ladies were assigned the room right next door to ours. We were told that we could move into our room but when we arrived with our gear the room was locked. I then had to play the game of hide and seek. When I found one of the four inhabitants I was told that the other lady had the key. When I found the other lady, she told me that one of the other girls had the key and so... on.... and.... on. I wondered if they knew the hardship they were placing on us?

I always find myself surprised when the behavior of a person is out of tune with the event or place. In this case I expected people living in a spiritual place to act in a more loving manner. The whole atmosphere of a spiritual environment should reflect the spiritual teachings of the teacher, the Guru. But just because a person travels to a holy place does not mean they are necessarily already a holy person. They simply wish to be.

Those who come to visit Bhagavan have many different motives and personalities. Sometimes the visitors are more interested in seeking out the para-normal, the sensationalism of Sai Baba, and are not really interested in practicing His stringent rules of selfless

39

love.

We had arrived just in time for Christmas. Christmas time at Prasanthi is special to Christians because Sai Baba celebrates the birth of Christ and gives extra attention to those who come at this time. This magical moment re-creates some of the spiritual fervor that early disciples and followers of Jesus must have felt.

Christmas Satsang and Carol practice starts about 10 days before Christmas. Each day there is a special guest speaker at satsang who shares his experiences with the foreigners. On one of these occasions I heard a talk given by Nassim Mishaan, known as Nate to most of us.

"In all the years I have come, each time the experience is different, never the same, always unique. I have come to the Divine Presence more than fifty times and the greatest miracle I have witnessed is the transformation He operates in us. His slow but steady transformation which does occur from one day to the other. We must become aware of this process of transformation occurring within us.

"We come to see Him, to see His leela, and His materializations but that is only the external part. The true sense of the trip is to see His Divine Presence and go within ourselves and realize who we are. We are not the body, we are the super-consciousness. That is the real reason for this trip and with Swami's Grace we shall succeed.

"We must be conscious that He is the doer. He does it all. He takes us upwards, downwards, makes us laugh or cry, gives us life and makes us die. Yes, indeed! I actually had that experience.

"Some years ago, I was very sick in my country. I felt I was going to die. When I came to Prasanthi He called and asked me, *"How is your health?"* I told Him, "Swamiji, very bad, I was very, very sick." He replied, *"Sick, you died! I gave you back your life, I gave you a second life."*

"Let us take everything with happiness! I recall that the first time I came to India, I had a great yearning to find God. I had read a lot about India. I went to many saints and sages, but did not find what I was looking for.

"The last day in Delhi, I found a book "Sai Baba Man of Miracles" by Howard Murphet. I read it and told myself that I would like to meet Sai Baba. That was what I had been looking for but how was I to get to that little village?

"Finally I arrived at Puttaparthi. I stayed there for three weeks. In the morning, a day before leaving, at darshan, Swami spoke to me and said, *"I will see you in the afternoon."* In the afternoon, He came to where I was and called all those who were sitting around me but not me! I was very angry. A friend told me, "Why are you angry? He told you He would see you and He did. I became more angry. I told myself not only didn't He call but now He was playing tricks with me.

"The following day He came near me and said, *"GO, Go to the interview."* I flew! I was the only foreigner He called that day. Swami spoke a lot in Telugu and then He moved His hand and materialized a ring. I was sitting in the back. He showed the ring to everyone and then He called me and put it on my finger. I started crying like a baby. He then told me many, many things. I asked His permission to return. He told me, *"Yes, many, many, many times."*

"We must realize that He is OMNIPRESENT, OMNISCIENT, and OMNIPOTENT. We are here because He called us. He brought every one of us here. This is what we must understand. Let us make the most of this opportunity. Eventually we shall be His messengers. Let us be happy with all our heart, let us be happy. Jai Sai Ram!"

Christmas Eve Darshan was one of the most touching I have ever experienced. We were all seated, waiting for Swami to come out, it rained heavily but no-one left. The soaked devotees dressed in their finest attire sat reverently in the darshan grounds waiting for "their" Dear Sai to appear.

When you sit along - side thousands of people sharing together such an intense spiritually charged moment, your heart has no choice but to stir at the sight of Our Beloved Sai.

The rain was an addition to this year's special Christmas atmosphere. It required a little something more from each of us. And because of our sacrifice there was an unspoken feeling of unity. We each had to endure a common problem... the uncomfortable condition in the rain. Here we sat, thousands of devotees in the rain, all of one mind and purpose, to wait for Sai Baba. This action increased our feeling of unity and love for Him.

It made me feel that in my small way, I was giving something to Our Lord, making some small sacrifice. He gives and gives and gives to each of us in so many ways, so often, so much. His act of giving creates within me the desire to give to Him. It was this very special feeling that was transferred from Him to me and back again that day. It was this bond of love that was intensified by all who attended and energized this magnificent Christmas Darshan in the rain.

It was still raining when Swami appeared on the verenda. I looked towards the sky to see if the rain would stop. I didn't want Our Dear Lord to get wet but the rain does not stop Him from going to His devotees. How sad, I felt when I saw Him walking in the rain, but He glowed like the sun, in His radiant orange robe and shining warm smile of Love. He looked at all of us sitting like wet ducks on a pond and gestured in a teasing manner asking us, "Why are you sitting in the rain?" He knows that when it's time for darshan, no one will leave, especially on Christmas Eve.

"Come just one step forward, I shall take a hundred towards you. Shed just one tear, I shall wipe a hundred from your eyes. I bless only thus! May your Ananda (bliss) grow." Sathya Sai Speaks 4, p. 36

As He came near I raised my hand extending the letters of the devotees from home and said, "Swami?" Asking Him in an unspoken tone did He wish to take them. He approached me, took the letters and smiled with loving sweetness. The Love He gives to us can heal all our wounds. How many times this year I had thought how will my next meeting with Sai be? Will He respond to me after He sent me from the interview room? Had I earned His grace again? How very much I had anticipated this first encounter. There could be no Christmas Gift that compared with the one He just gave me.

After Sai's darshan the grounds were empty each devotee dripping with love, never mind the water. The first task at hand was to change into dry clothes. When Robert came into the room, he shared his darshan with me. He spoke of nothing but the Love that he felt as Sai stood by Him swaying and gesturing with His hand. The familiar hand movement of a small circle, drawn in the air, which appears to us that He is purifying us and the atmosphere.

While I was in the room, I glanced down and on the table my eyes caught a passage in Sanathana Sarathi that said, *"When My rain touches you, I am cleansing you, Think of Me!"*

All the people returned for bhajans in clean dry clothes, the weather was co-operating, the rain had stopped. Swami had the boys set out his red chair on the veranda. As He was the main attraction, all eyes focused on Him. The Christmas Choir began to sing and as if in response the rain came again, more gently. Swami was so happy, moving his hand to the beat of the Christmas music sung by the choir. The harder it rained the faster Sai moved His hand. My, I thought, "He's cleansing us more." All the dry clothes were soaked again.

Swami appeared to be playing with us. His mood was joyful. When the Christmas songs concluded, Sai requested us to sing some bhajans, never mind the rain. He seemed to be enjoying the game!

This Christmas Eve inspired me to write an article on "Christmas Darshan in the Rain." I felt good because this article was printed in the Christmas Sanathana issue. It was a sign for me that Baba approved of my writing this year.

Christmas morning in the ashram is very different from the traditional event of running to see what Santa Clause has deposited under the tree. Instead we rise early, and as dawn emerges we gather to see Our Lord standing on the balcony giving His traditional Christmas Blessing.

All the foreign devotees form a procession and walk around the ashram singing Christmas Carols and ending up below Sai Baba's balcony. There we stand, filling the Mandir courtyard with thousands of tiny flickering lights. Each candle we hold is symbolic of our own little contribution of light to His world that so much needs His spiritual light.

Swami's Love energy made me feel high and my soul felt lighter as I meandered in a contemplative mood back to my room. Then there was the usual morning hustle and bustle with the chores and readiness to meet Our Lord Sai Jesus at Christmas Darshan.

There was a Christmas gift left for me under His tree this year, an unexpected surprise. As I entered the line-up area, I was asked to join five foreign devotees to pass out the Christmas Prasad. It was the first time that foreigners were allowed to pass out prasad on the darshan grounds. As if this was not enough joy for my heart to hold; He gave yet another gift, that of being seated in the front line right across from the veranda. Box seat viewing! This would ensure our easy accessibility when the appropriate time came to pass out the prasad.

I sat basking in the morning sun peering at the interview-room door hoping to catch the first glimpse of Sai as He came out to give us darshan. I was 'thanking Him' for the good fortune of having the best seat possible when the Seva Dal that invited me to join this group was now asking me to move to the rear because the seat was needed for someone else. 'Well' I thought 'thanks for the momentary experience!' I remembered the Sai Saying, "Joy is a brief interlude between two sorrows!" I got up and moved.

The boys from Sai Baba's school entertained us with song and music. They played and sang like God's Cherubs in this celestial like setting. To witness this is the greatest way to spend Christmas for any Christ minded person. When the time came to distribute the prasad, I knew that for me this was an honor because it represented giving food to His devotees, a chance to serve the masses of mankind the prasad of LOVE in His Divine Presence and under His direct guidance. I hoped that this was a sign of my future. Being able to fill each outstretched hand in need with His Sweet Love.

Swami stood on the veranda steps directing this part of His play. As we walked back and forth in front of Him,

He would instruct the boys to bring more and remind us if we overlooked an area, making sure that none of His flock were being forgotten. After all the prasad had been distributed there was none left for those who did the serving. But after we sat down, Swami who knows and provides for all of us, had another box of sweets brought out to be given to us. He not only feeds those who are served; He feeds those who do the serving as well.

When I am in Swami's presence, time seems to stop. I was amazed that one and a half hours had passed. This Christmas morning He lavished so much Love on each one of us.

Another lesson He taught me on this Christmas Day happened in the evening when Sai Baba held His Christmas Discourse and a play was presented by children from overseas. I arrived early hoping to get a chair. Only two remained and I sat in one but the chair was far from the stage. After the big hall doors at the side opened I moved my chair to sit in the rear of the front arch.

When Swami arrived crowds of people came as if from no-where and surrounded the chairs. Since I was in the last row they were leaning on me. One of the girls next to me leaned so heavily that I requested her to move since I have a bad back and was in pain. She spoke rudely and did not move. It was hot. I decided to try a little experiment. I closed my eyes and meditated on this young girl and her family standing around my chair. I kept sending Swami's love through me to them and soon they moved and the girl started talking to me in a very friendly manner. I could now listen to Sai's discourse in more comfort. He often reminds us that love is the greatest power.

During the break between the discourse and the beginning of the play, some women in the very front row of the chairs got up. One of them, a stranger, looked at me and said, "Do you want to sit in my chair because I am leaving?" "Yes, thank you," I replied, and so I had a front row view of the children's play. I remembered that this morning I had a front row seat and was asked to move to the rear. This afternoon, I had a rear seat and was asked to move to the front. I wondered what this was about?

Christmas as I used to know it has lost all meaning for me. I enjoy being with Sai on this holy day instead of celebrating in a material way. I realize it's the only way I wish to celebrate the holiness of Jesus's Birthday in my future.

So much had happened since we arrived two days ago. My! How He showered me with His love! How could I ever doubt His constant Presence? Six months before our trip to India, our children requested that we travel through the Far East instead of going to Europe because of all the terrorist activities. We agreed. It was a little unsettling because four devotees we knew, had been on a hi-jacked plane. We used our common sense and traveled via Singapore. On his very first darshan Robert had a front row seat. Sai Baba walked to him, took the letters he held written by devotees at home. Then Robert knelt up and said, "Thank you Sai for getting us here safely." Baba replied, "Not Hijacked!" We had forgotten about our concern at the time we booked six months ago but Swami knew it all.

All these small incidents soon become more than coincidences, especially when they occur so frequently. Once I heard Swami say, *"If you don't see God... who moved?"* I just loved that statement. It's so vivid. God lives within my heart and is there permanently. It is I who choose in my heart to visit him by consciously seeking His counsel. But many times I act without inquiring within first. When I feel as if Swami is not answering my prayer, or as if He is ignoring me, then I ask myself, "Who moved?"

Sometimes the presence of God in our lives is overlooked because our awareness is not finely tuned. I've heard people say, that they are not aware of God doing things for them, that they control their own life.

"You consider the world as very near, as around you and behind you; but when you have to point out the Lord, you show Him far away from you, up and above, or at a vast distance. This is a mistake. The Lord is near; the world is far. You are believing that it is the other way as you are afraid of the truth and you like to deceive yourself. Sathya Sai Speaks 2, p. 166

When I'm visiting Sai at Prasanthi Nilayam and I'm away from all the distracting influences in my life it's easier to tune into His Divine Intervention. Especially when the circumstances are dramatized from the norm. I am able to see His will being expressed mostly when it is accentuated by giving me more or less outward attention. It's also interesting to note, that it takes more awareness to ignore someone than to casually see them. He only appears, to avoid or ignore me.

Another example of His Divine Will acting in my life came on New Year's Day. We were all lined up to enter the Poornachandra for His afternoon Discourse. The crowds were rather un-disciplined and it was impossible for the Seva Dals to handle the large numbers of devotees who had come during this festival time. I have never had a front row seat in the auditorium because they are mostly saved for special guests. But this day I was to become a "special person." The head lady volunteer, Mataji, was choosing some of the VIP families to go in for special seating and suddenly her finger pointed to me. I didn't wait for her to change her mind. Good fortune was shining on me and I scurried to the Poornachandra Hall. Some of my friends were sitting in the front row, squeezing together they made room for me.

After Sai's Discourse, He entertained us with a Musical Contest given by His students. Each performance excelled the previous one. I had to remind myself that these contestants were Sai Baba students. Their performance was very professional. I became absorbed in the mystical sound of the music and the vision of Sai in His regal chair, drinking in the splendor of the moment.

After hours of sitting on the floor my back was screaming out for attention. The musical program was almost concluded when the last contestant came on stage. Our host kept the greatest musician till last. Angelic music filled the air and the heavenly sounds stirred those sleepy, tired souls to sit up and again become attentive. As Sai swayed His head from side to side, my eyes met His and soon I became a part of His Bliss. I was removed from body consciousness, the aches and pains were no longer there. I was "Blissed Out!"

"The beaming joy on the faces of this vast multitude is the food that I live upon; I am refreshed when you are happy and content. My thirst is quenched by the joy which lights up your eyes. Your Ananda is My Ahara. I do not feel like talking to you at all, for I desire only to communicate to you My Joy and to get into communion with your Joy. This mutual fulfilment is the essential thing; talking and listening are subsidiary." Sathya Sai speaks 4, p. 332

Front row darshan was very scarce on this trip. I kept drawing numbers between 20 and 30. Only twice since my first darshan did I have a first row, once when He took my note asking if Donna was alive and well. Another day I received Padnamaskar and offered my manuscript to Swami and He said gently, *"wait... wait."* It was not what I had wanted to hear but His message acknowledged that I had a manuscript. I was grateful.

I kept hearing the voice inside saying, "Do not pick numbers, sit on the chairs, when I need you, I will call. You no longer need constant attention. You have matured. I have taken your letters, signed your pictures, spoken with you often, and given you Padnamaskar on many visits. Now it is time for you to sit in the back and let a new devotee take your place." As the remaining days dwindled, the pressure to get close to Baba increased. I came later and sat in the rear, and did not pick numbers, as He directed me from inside. I would do this for as long as I could but watching from a long distance was painful, especially when I remembered all the attention He had given me before. I wanted His charm shining directly on me. When I could no longer bear the back seat, I would go in the darshan lines and take a chit. I had hoped that the message from my inner voice was untrue. Perhaps today, I'll get close to the front but even when I put my hand in the bag of numbers to draw for the row, I'd get the last number. He was helping to wean me from the front row to the rear.

"You think that I pay attention only to those who sit in front, but, I see all and I am with all, wherever they may be. Only those who have been blessed will know, not the rest."

This avoidance action taken by Swami made me angry. I was feeling rejected and ignored again. How the emotions waver! "Why the anger," I inquired? "Why am I mad?" I looked within and again saw my original feeling that I started with on this trip, expecting some recognition for writing this manuscript, even though my daily intention stated "All I do I offer to you." And now when I am here, being tested, I find that what I said was not actually what I wanted. How did this impurity slip into my original motive?

It's easy to make a promise or statement of good-will but when we are called upon to act in the manner that we promised, it calls for an additional inner strength. Here I was faced with my own anger because I didn't get what I wanted. And yet I had told Swami everyday that year, that I surrendered my action and their fruits to Him. Well

52

now I must live up to my word. I removed the anger.

After the game of chit drawing, I finally understood what happened to me on Christmas Day concerning my seating. Remember, I had a front row seat assigned to me and then I was asked to go to the back. During the afternoon, discourse and play, I was called forward by a stranger asking me to come to the front and take her seat. It was a very effective maneuver.

This experience confirmed my inward message. I had a front row, meaning I had so much attention in previous trips and now, I was asked to go to the back and give someone else a chance. I should remain in the rear and when He wanted me, He would call me. This was certainly the theme for my trip. What a grand teacher I have!

About five days before we were to leave, Robert and I were sitting in our Prasanthi apartment looking at the damage of large cracks and water stains that came from a huge water storage tank above our unit. This damage happened during Swami's Sixtieth Birthday. We are on the top floor and the tank was above us. It leaked profusely and flooded the roof which put pressure and leakage on our ceiling and walls. We wanted to get our unit fixed but knew that it would need to be supervised, and hadn't a clue how we could do it.

As we sat discussing this issue there was a knock on our door. It was Bob Reinhart. He came in and said, "If you want any work to be done on your apartment, I'd like to take it on as a service project." I thought the angel of mercy had descended upon us! Oh Swami, how sweet you are!! Of course we said, **"YES!"** We told Bob his timing was Divine because we were just talking about this very thing and the Lord sent him to our door. There was none more capable to supervise this project than Bob.

We took his advice and in the few remaining days had the cement work done to place our beds upon. We designed the beds to be used as a wall sofa in the daytime. We spoke with Richard and Michelle Kaplowitz who recently had there room done, asking for their advice. They told us where to shop for the tiles and bathroom fixtures and what mistakes can take place and how to guard against any defective supplies.

We had a day and a half to spend in Bangalore shopping for supplies. We knew our time for shopping was extremely limited compared to the usual time it takes to select and arrange for supplies in India. That's why we knew God's Hand was preparing the way because every detail went smoothly and the chores were finished in one day.

We didn't receive an interview nor did I give Sai Baba the manuscript but in every other way He pampered us. Robert had an excellent darshan just before we left. Swami stood right in front of him when bhajans began with the chanting of three Om's. He smiled so lovingly to Robert, came to him and took our note asking for permission to leave on Friday. Baba allowed Robert to hold His hand and kiss His feet.

Mr. Narsimhan, the editor of the Sanathana Sarathi said he wanted to see us after bhajans and we went to his apartment. He wanted to show us the article I wrote in the new issue of the monthly journal. There was also a picture of Swami giving darshan on Christmas day and guess who was sitting there, in front of Him, non other than Robert. He had to get in the act somewhere and the Lord assisted him!

The day before we left was Pongal Day, Thursday January 14, 1987 Sai Baba gave a Discourse and distributed the Sports Awards for the recent Sports Day Activities. Sai's Discourse to His students on the value of sports, was illuminating and inspiring.

"The reason for the increased disease in the world is no peace of mind. Today's students do not know peace of mind. If we examine the reason for this state of mind it is bad habits and food.

Man has lost his discrimination of what is good and what is bad for him. He eats anything to satisfy his hunger. It is better to have hunger than to eat what is not good for you.

Games and sports are good for your health and concentration. But today sports are converted into a business. Money becomes the objective. The moment that games or music is turned into a business, man's health will deteriorate.

What is the purpose of art and sports games? It is to achieve a good name and reputation for our country, but money is harming this. Money comes and gos. What's important is the sacrifice, concentration, patriotism and devotion you learn from sports. We should not be selfish and arrogant people.

Our youth is selling itself today and this reaps self-destruction. Through sports you can control your thoughts and develop concentration but you must obey the rules and regulations of sports. Football and volleyball need team work. Forget one's own self and give the ball to the one who is near the goal.

If your mind and body is strong then there is nothing that you cannot do. You will get the Love of God. If we achieve the Love of God we will be able to achieve anything in the world."

LOVE - SACRIFICE - UNITY

"Nowhere in the world is Christmas celebrated in the manner in which it is done in Prasanthi Nilayam. People belonging to different countries, different faiths and different cultures, coming together to adore God and celebrate this festival in such a holy atmosphere cannot be found anywhere else. Love, Sacrifice and Unity should be your watchwords."

DIVINE DISCOURSE

There is a Creator for this marvellous and beautiful cosmos, consisting of moving and unmoving objects. He is Omniscient, Omnipotent and Omnipresent. He has been worshipped as God by many names and in many forms by various people.

Adored by Muslims as Allah,
As Jehovah by Christians
As the Lotus-eyed Lord by Vaishnavites,
As Sambhu by Saivites,
The One who confers health and wealth,
Revere Him as the one Supreme Omni-Self.

Unity, fellow-feeling and devotion are essential for every human being. To promote these sacred qualities in mankind, some great souls sought to establish different religions. Religion is not a restrictive concept. Religion is

57

intended to develop the human personality and indicate the basic guidelines for right living. Religion brings out the humanness in man and enables him to live in harmony with his fellow-men. It provides the link between the individual and the Divine. It demonstrates the unity that underlies the diversity in the world.

Love, Sacrifice, Service and Righteousness are the four limbs of Religion. Religion brings out the divine and sublime feelings in man and makes him serve society. It evokes all that is great, blissful and good in men and demonstrates the unity of mankind.

It is supremely unfortunate that Religion, which has such high and sacred objectives, is construed and practised in a narrow way and propagated as a narrow creed.

Religion is like an undercurrent that sustains the whole of humanity. The founders of religions, with a view to spreading the subtle secrets of religious faith, laid down certain rules of conduct and conveyed their message to the people.

Buddhism declared that Truth and Non-violence are the basic requisites for getting rid of delusions and achieving purity in life.

Christianity proclaimed that all are children of God and should have fraternal feelings towards each other. Jesus declared: "All are one, be alike to everyone."

According to Islam, all are members of one family in spiritual terms. It regarded prayer as the best means of ensuring peace and security in society.

Emperor Manu declared: "One must be prepared to sacrifice his body for his community and his community for the sake of the nation." Manu's Dharmasastra laid down the welfare of society as most important.

The Upanishads declared: "The Divine has myriad eyes and myriad feet." All eyes are God's; all feet are His; all hands are His. This was the message of the Upanishads. In this manner, the Upanishads emphasised the oneness of humanity.

For man, it is the collective concept that is fundamental and not individualism. No one can live in this world all by himself. He has to cultivate the sense of community if he wishes to live in peace and happiness. "Let us live together; let us struggle together; let us grow together in joy and harmony." This was the teaching of the Vedas.

It is evident that in this way all religions propagated unity for promoting the well-being of society. The welfare of the world is bound up with the well-being of society. Self-Realisation and Self-Knowledge can be got only through social involvement. Unfortunately, society today is riddled with strife, chaos and conflict.

All religions preached the greatness of spiritual purity. All religions called upon people to adhere to the path of Truth. They also taught that good qualities are essential for man. Thus, when the essence of all religions is one and the same, when all the scriptures proclaim the same truth, when the goal of all human efforts is one, where is the basis for any differences? The paths are varied, but the destination is one and the same.

It is a sign of man's degradation that in spite of these truths, he indulges in conflicts and agitations on account of religious differences. When there is a downpour, the water that comes down is pure. The rain falls on mountains, plains, rivers, the sea and so on. According to the region through which the rain water passes, its name and form undergo changes. Because of these variations, it should not be thought that the water itself is different.

Based on the teachings of the founders of different faiths, having regard to the requirements of the time and circumstance of particular countries, and keeping in view the specific needs of the people concerned, certain rules and regulations were laid down. On this account, one faith should not be considered superior and another inferior. Man's primary duty is to bear in mind these sacred truths and practice them in his life.

Truth is a fundamental principle. All religions have declared that no one should break his plighted word. That man should honour his pledges, that he should regard his words as his life-breath, that keeping his promises is the greatest treasure, this was the primary teaching of the great Law-giver, Emperor Manu (author of the Dharmasastra).

Plato was the foremost among the disciples of Socrates. Aristotle was a disciple of Plato. Alexander was a pupil of Aristotle. Plato commended a system of polity based on morality, righteousness, mutual forbearance as conducive to the well-being of society. He attached the greatest importance to Truth, Beauty, and Goodness as the basic virtues. In the Vedas these three qualities have been described as Sathyam, Sivam, Sundaram. Thus, though

60

different words are used, their essential purport is the same. Spiritual discipline consists in recognising the unity underlying the apparent diversity and realising divinity.

Bharatiya culture has always upheld the supremacy of faith in God. Bharatiya culture was based on the view that there is nothing in the world which is not permeated by the Divine. From a stone to a diamond, from a blade of grass to a blooming lotus, from an ant to an elephant, everything was regarded as a manifestation of the Divine. Bharatiya culture upheld the view that love should not be confined to human beings, but should be extended to all beings and objects in creation. Ignoramuses who have not understood this great truth speak disparagingly of Bharatiyas as people who worship stones, trees, serpents and the like. In the eyes of Bharatiyas, every object is a creation of God. "Sarvam Khaluidam Brahma" ("All this is Brahman"), "Sarvam Vishnumayam Jagat" ("The cosmos is permeated by Vishnu"). These vedantic declarations proclaim the same truth. You cannot find in any other country a universal, all-embracing sacred declaration of this kind. This contains the broad concept of social justice. You cannot see in any other country such a sacred view.

Although all religions have preached this truth of oneness and equality, selfish persons, for their own ends, have interpreted them in narrow terms and promoted strife and discord between different people.

One who is merely well versed in the scriptures cannot be called a "Pandita" (a person with knowledge and wisdom). Even a master of the Vedas, sastras and puranas cannot be esteemed a Pandita. Scholarship alone does not make a man a Pandita. Mastery of language does not confer this title. "Pandits are those who see all with an equal eye," says the Gita. Only the person who has this vision of equality can be esteemed a Pandita. Hence, we should look upon all religions with equal respect. No religion should be criticised or reviled. One should imbibe the sweet essence in all religions.

The essence of all religions is the principle of Oneness, the principle of Love. When you cultivate this principle of love, there is no room for hatred.

Today religion is regarded as the cause for all the conflict, violence and bitterness in the world. But, religion is not the cause. Selfish minds are responsible for all the conflict. Are there not conflicts in countries with only one religion? People in Iran and Iraq profess the same Islamic faith. What is the reason for the conflict between them? What is the reason for conflicts between countries which profess Christianity? In Bharat, all are Bharatiyas. But why is there discord amongst them? When we examine this question deeply, we find that religions are not the real reason for these conflicts. Only selfish minds are the cause. Wearing the garb of religion, these selfish persons are inciting conflicts among the people.

Embodiments of Divine Love! If you desire to secure genuine peace in the world, you should not have any antipathy towards religion. You must hold morality as superior to your community. You must cherish good feelings as more important than religious beliefs. Mutual regard, equalmindedness and forebearance are basic qualities necessary for every human being. Only the person with these three qualities can be regarded as a true man. It is essential that everyone should cultivate these three sacred qualities. How did differences arise within each religion? After the passing of the founders of these religions, the followers violated the teachings of the founders and quarrelled among themselves on account of their selfish interests. With the passage of time, schisms developed in each religion and separate sects were formed. This is the result of individual, selfish motives and not the fault of the original founders.

People must first of all get rid of self-interest and self-centeredness. They must develop love, forebearance and compassion. They must try to live harmoniously. Only then can we claim to be lovers of peace in the nation and of the well-being of the world.

"Service" should be the guiding principle. There should be no room for any kind of differences in rendering service. When you wish to serve society, you must be prepared to sacrifice your individual and communal interests. Such sacrifice alone will sublimate one's life. The Vedas have emphatically declared that immortality can be attained only through sacrifice and not by any other means.

To propagate this message of equalmindedness, the army of Sai devotees must prepare themselves. Today, in Prasanthi Nilayam, members belonging to a variety of faiths have come together. They speak different languages. They belong to diverse traditions. But all of them have a single belief, a single ideal that is Love.

The Christmas festival is celebrated in many countries with a lot of fanfare, merriment and riotous festivities. You *should note one thing. Nowhere in the world is Christmas celebrated in the manner in which it is done in Prasanthi Nilayam. People belonging to different countries, different faiths and different cultures, coming together to adore God and celebrate this festival in such a holy atmosphere cannot be found anywhere else. This should spread to all countries.*

Christmas is celebrated in America, Germany, Italy and other countries. But in what manner? By sumptuous eating, drinking and dancing and wasting time. Here also you indulge in drink. But what is it you are drinking: You are drinking Pure Divine Love. It is this Love that you must offer to the world.

Don't entertain religious difference of any kind. Put into practice the message you receive here and share the bliss of your experience with others. Preaching to others is not enough.

Everyone should develop devotion and dedication. Life without devotion is worthless. If one does not show his gratitude to the Creator, of what avail is his life? Should you not show some gratitude to the Lord who has provided such infinite benefits through Nature and the elements? Gratitude should be the life-breath of a man.

The founders of religions experienced these truths and propagated them as ideals for mankind. You must wholeheartedly live up to these teachings. Mere reading of the Bible or reciting the Quran, repeating the Bhagavad Gita or chanting the Granth Saheb is not meritorious. The basic teachings in each of these texts have to be put into practice in daily life.

Socrates used to gather young men around him and expound to them how to enquire into what is transient and what is permanent. He told them that only those who have devotion and dedication are entitled to wield power. A ruler should adhere to Truth and show his gratitude to God. Puffed up with ego, he should not forget the Almighty. Those who did not relish Socrates teachings brought charges against him. When he was sentenced to death, he chose to die by drinking the cup of hemlock from the hands of his disciples. Before his death, he told his disciples that no one should die leaving an undischarged debt behind him. He told a disciple that he owed a cock to a friend and asked him to discharge that obligation.

Prophet Mohamed, likewise, told his disciples before his passing that the money he owed to a camel driver should be paid before his end came. The discharging of one's debts is regarded as a pious obligation for every Bharatiya. Harischandra sacrificed everything for the sake of honoring his plighted word.

It will be seen that all religions have emphasized the greatness of Truth, Sacrifice and Unity. Learn to live in love and harmony with all the members of your society. This is the basic teaching of Christianity and Islam. Guru Nanak favoured community prayers in preference to individual prayer in isolation. When all people join in unison to pray to God, their prayers will melt the heart of God. In a large gathering there must be at least one who prays with a pure heart. That prayer will reach God. Hence, devotees should take part in community bhajans. They should participate in community service and involve themselves in the life of the community. This is the noblest path.

Cultivate love. Love is the form of the Divine and God can be realised only through love. Of all the myriad names given to God, the one which is most to be cherished is Sat-Chit-Ananda (Being-Awareness-Bliss). 'Sat' represents Truth. 'Chit' represents Jnana (wisdom). Where Sat and Chit are present, "Ananda" (Bliss) is bound to be present. As God is Truth, He has to be realised through Truth. As God is Jnana, He has to be realised through the path of knowledge. As He is Bliss, He has to be realised through Truth. Follow the path of Love and achieve the goal of Unity. Banish all differences. This is the supreme message for you today.

Embodiments of Divine Love! Wherever you may be, in whatever country, do not give room for religious differences. Do not give up religion. Get rid of differences based on religion. Adhere to your faith and your traditions. When differences between religions are given up, love will develop in you. When love grows, you can have a direct vision of God. Without love, verbal prayers are of no avail. Realise that the love that is present in everyone is common to all. It is love that has brought you all together. It is the cord of love that has bound all of you. It is the unifier, the motivator and the bringer of joy to all. Therefore, develop love.

Sanathana Sarathi,
January 1991 p. 18

DEATH AND DYING

We were exhausted when we arrived in St. Louis and were greeted by our family. It wasn't long before Craig told us the distressing news about our parents. Robert's mother and my father were both seriously ill and reported by their respective doctors as dying. It was a sad homecoming to hear about both of our parents suffering with a terminal illness. Robert's mother, Nadine had been ill with a congenital heart disorder. She had been struggling with the various stages of this illness for several years and had been confined to her wheel chair and oxygen assistance for breathing.

The miraculous story about my father, Sylvester, is in my first book. He was cured of cancer by Swami in January 1985. It was **exactly** three years ago to the day when dad had taken Vibhuthi that was materialized by Swami and given to our son Craig while in darshan. Craig promptly sent it home.

67

In January 1985, dad had surgery and the doctors discovered cancer in his liver, colon, and stomach. Dad's condition was serious and he was given a few months to live. He could not eat any food and became weak and thin. But after taking Swami's vibhuthi his health improved and when the doctor re-examined him through exploratory surgery they found all the cancer to be benign. His appetite increased, his strength returned and his life resumed to a normal lifestyle. He was 77 years old and shot his age in golf. It was a miracle that was confirmed by Swami. Now, I heard that he was in the same condition again three years later. Dad did not change his diet or lifestyle, so the original condition that caused the illness prevailed again.

Sai says, *It should be noted that all the problems and troubles of man are due to the fact that he does not know how to make proper use of his body. Hence he becomes an easy prey to sorrow and disease.*

"When you clean your house daily and go on dumping the sweepings in one place, it will grow into a big heap. Likewise, when you go on dumping into your body various kinds of food so many times per day, your body, though insentient will grow like the heap of garbage." Indian Culture and Spirituality p. 18

Both parents were in two different hospitals located an hour away from each other. Dad was in a hospital near the airport which is about an hour from our house so we decided to visit him before going home and since it was late we would have to visit Bob's mom in the morning.

Dad was glad to see us. The doctor had run some tests and the cancer was active again. He appeared hopeless and exhausted because of his battle with cancer which started about 12 years ago. He seemed tired of fighting for life. Cancer and its devastating symptoms were no stranger to mom and dad. In the previous years he had had a cancerous kidney removed by surgery and two colon operations, plus chemotherapy treatments. He also took Laetrile in a treatment center in Mexico. He had fought a gallant fight but appeared apathetic. Who could blame him? He had physically suffered much too much in this life. The doctor was sending him home because there was no way dad would consent to another operation. The cancer was too extensive.

This news, and the sight of mom and dad was depressing. When someone we love is afflicted and you are not able to fix it, it saddens our spirit. There is a hopelessness that sinks into the heart and creates a "heavy heart." The greater our love for another; the more we ache. I loved mom and dad so very much and to see the threat of final separation and their longing to stay with each other just a little longer was almost unbearable.

I asked myself over and over, how would I respond under seemlier circumstances? I couldn't think about this very much because it made me too emotional and that was the last thing my parents needed now. I wanted to be a support to them as they had always been for me. I was at least comforted in the philosophy of life and death that Sai Baba had taught me.

He has stressed that our body is just temporary and our spiritual identity is the one that is permanent. I knew that my father's spiritual body would still live in the afterlife, and sometime we would meet again.

Even though our bodies are temporary, it is the only vehicle we have and it is needed to make the sojourn from man to God. We are very fortunate to have life on earth at the same time that God is here. Their are many souls waiting for this same opportunity. It is so easy to lose sight of our spiritual purpose and the added bonus of having God here to help us attain our spiritual goal. The only vehicle that we have is our body, and if we fill it full of disease we cannot be successful.

Baba says, *"The body undergoes various changes due to food and other living habits. Whatever the changes in the body, the individuality remains unchanged. The changes of name and form such as childhood, boyhood, manhood and old age pertain to the body and hence are illusory. You should not therefore consider the body as real and permanent at all. Nevertheless it is your duty to ensure that the body is not subjected to diseases and is maintained as a fit instrument. As long as you sail in this river of life, you must see to it that the boat of your body does not develop holes or leaks thereby preventing water from entering into the boat. The boat may be in water, but there should be no water in the boat. Remain in the world and attend to your duties, but don't allow worries to enter your mind and make your body susceptible to all kinds of diseases. Consider the body as only an instrument."* Indian Culture and Spirituality p. 21

Another reason for my uneasiness was the deterioration of my own body due to the fact that I was not eating properly. How often Swami has said to us not to eat sugar, salt, and fat. And yet, everything that tastes good has these ingredients. How my tongue loves to savor the culinary creations not only from America, but I'm hooked on foods from many countries. The tongue gets too much pleasure from eating.... and I'm blinded to the reality of self-destruction. How long can we satisfy the palate without paying the toll of sickness?

It was less than a week ago when I was in India and heard Sai Baba's Discourse on Pongal Day 1988.

*"Who can save you from your own fate? We are all born with a heavy garland around our neck. It is not visible to you at birth but nevertheless you are wearing a garland. This garland is giving you actions that come from your **own** past. The fruits that you are enjoying is from this invisible garland. They are based upon your own previous thoughts and actions. These thoughts and actions are sacred."*

I knew dad was working through some rough karma. I once was told by a devotee that Swami said, "Cancer can cancel karma quickly." That it must be because of the intense suffering, hardship and pain. The situation was a living hell for mom and dad. I was comforted in only two ways, that it would soon be over for him and his karma would be canceled.

Sai says, *"In the case of the human body, you are bound to reap the fruits of the good or bad thoughts and actions which you sow as seeds. You are sure to have cent percent*

return. As you sow, so you reap. This is an immutable law."
Indian Culture and spirituality p. 14

The next morning we visited Robert's mom, Nadine. She too looked weak and her illness was diagnosed as Congenital Heart Disease. For the past two years, her life had changed drastically. Because of the failing heart, and a slight stroke, she was confined to her apartment alone, because Dad Bruce died 8 years before.

Mom Bruce loved life and children. She had fun shopping, sewing dolls clothes, belonging to clubs and enjoying her family and friends. This was a woman who went somewhere every day because she did not like to be confined. Now she was faced with the three greatest obstacles of her life...... illness, loss of husband, and finally staying home.

It is apparent that when we become seniors we are confronted with tremendous hardship, even though we dream that life should become easier as we grow older. But in truth, the karma continues, even in old age, and I see the older people confronted with the greatest challenges that life can offer especially when they are physically more vulnerable. They suffer old age, illness, death of spouse, financial insecurity, and loneliness.

God is not easy on us. He wants us to detach from the world and focus on Him. His greatest concern is with our spiritual well-being. Any desire that we have, even when we are old, He forces us to experience it until we finally "let go." The very thing we want can become too unbearable or too "hot" to hold on too.

He says, *"Dahyati iti dehah - That which is burnt is called the body. This is the derivative meaning of the word Deha - body. It is a matter of common knowledge that the body is burnt after death. But even when it is alive, the body experiences burning due to worries."* Indian Culture and Spirituality p. 11

Mom Bruce could not breathe and the doctor had her on oxygen. She had been fighting for breath for the past several years. She would get very short winded. I would see her gasp for air whenever she tried to do anything whether it was eating or dressing etc. She would end up panting. How horrible, her very breath was being snuffed away.

I prayed to Our Lord to end their misery soon.

My dad could not eat and was literally starving to death. While he was at home we used all the services that Medicare provided for the home patient such as visiting nurses etc. We also used Hospice. These people are 'angels' in disguise. Their re-assurance and sympathy helped to calm our fears. My mom also lost thirty-five pounds because of the stress and worry of watching dad die.

Towards the end, dad was too difficult for us to handle at home so he had to go back to the hospital. He didn't want to go; and I didn't want to tell him. It was excruciating for me to tell dad but it was far more severe for him to hear and accept. How does one leave one's earthly home after many years, knowing one will never be there again? It is a smoother transition if we prepare early in life by viewing all here as temporary.

I said, "Dad, you are getting so weak and your large frame is too heavy for any of us to lift you onto the toilet chair that is next to your bed. The doctor said it was time for you to go into the hospital; you will receive better care." He knew what I was saying was true but he still mumbled that he did not want to go. I felt like I was sentencing him to prison because of his dislike of hospitals. Dad was not speaking anymore because of weakness. But he could communicate through nods and gestures.

I spoke, "Dad, do me one favor after you die. I know you don't understand Sai Baba but when you die, you will be able to travel with your spirit body. Please promise me that you will go to see Him in India and investigate His Divinity." Our eyes met as he nodded his head, "yes". My father's character was honorable; I knew that I could count on his promise.

Dad signed a Living Will and decided not to have intravenous feeding. He wanted nothing to prevent or linger his death. Sai Baba had spared dad from any physical pain which was an enormous gift from Sai.

My father and mother were both very spiritual, and prayer sustained them both. But my father had a fear of the unknown, of death. It showed on his grief - stricken face, and I didn't know how to alleviate it, even though I spoke to him about Sai Baba's teachings on death. My words did not seem to help very much.

Sai says, *"You cannot take up the threads of spiritual discipline all of a sudden after retiring from active service. You cannot learn spiritual practices when you are physically debilitated and overwhelmed by the approach of death. How can a man think of God, his Savior, when he himself is overcome by sorrow at the need to depart from this world and when all around him, his kith and kin, are weeping and wailing loud and long?"* Sathya Sai Speaks, volume 9.

His fear forced me to deal with my own fears on death and illness and gave me my first real perception on the process of dying from a degenerating disease. It was awful. But this observation did create for me a motive for keeping clean food habits.

Swami said, *"Students! The world today is simmering with discord and violence. Peace and security are absent. Fear stalks the land everywhere. To get rid of fear, you have to acquire fearlessness ("Abhayatvam"). How is it to be got? When you reduce desires and attachments.* Sanathana Sarathi April 1993, p. 107

I stuck really close to Swami. I wanted to soothe my father's and my mother's fears, as best I could. Even though I was scared too, I had Baba. I would grab His hand and hold it tight every time I entered the hospital. Hospitals would drive me crazy, I would walk down a corridor and I could feel people's suffering. I was too sensitive and Swami was teaching me to stay balanced and detached. He was giving me many opportunities to deal with my own fears as I lived this moment with mom and dad. I knew the last thing they needed was my fear so I drew on Our Lord's strength. But after I left mom and dad; sometimes I too would fall apart and cry. Robert and I each supported one another and we would lean heavily on Sai Baba.

Swami said in Kodai during the summer of 1992, *"I give you one problem, you solve it.... I send you ten more!"* He was so pleased with Himself, as he spoke. Joyful may be a better description, but it was obvious that He knew something more than we did. He continued, *"Why does God give you problems? Because when you have problems you YEARN for God. When you are happy and content you do not think of Him."*

Swami's childlike expression is what triggered my thinking. His emotional response was something like the pleasure a 3 or 4 year old has when he first rides a tricycle, "I did it, I did it!" That was how pleased He sounded as He spoke those words, *"I give you one problem, you solve it, I send you 10 more."*

The second thing that got my attention was the word YEARN. I was already familiar with our great need to yearn for the Lord, but I did not recognize the connection between power, pain and yearning. Our emotional response to pain and stress is stronger than our emotional response to joy. These intense feelings make a greater impact on our learning experience. The results are more permanent. The stronger the emotional response; the greater the remembrance. The greater the emotional impact; the more the thoughts stick! These types of experiences deepen and strengthen our relationship with our inner God.

Yearning stirs God's heart and our heart. It is this yearning that increases our love vibration, until the magical time when our soul has attained the Lord's level

76

of Love and we can merge with Him.

His words of wisdom and the emotion in which the statement was made increased my understanding on the objective of pain and suffering. God is **only** interested in bringing us home to Him, and liberating us from the cycle of birth and death. He wants to give us Bliss, and we in our ignorance cannot realize it! The importance of good children, a happy marriage, marvelous job, excellent health, prosperity, etc., etc., is a human goal, not necessarily a Divine one. It's not that He isn't happy about our human situation, He feels joy or sadness when we do, but His primary concern is our Spiritual Evolution. His duty to us is to remove all our ignorance and karma, as well as developing within us inner peace, not the temporary comfort of a peaceful, plush lifestyle! Let's face it: no one wants to hurt!

Dad's illness certainly gave me the opportunity to notice the temporary nature of man. I even felt a renewed urgency to achieve a healthier body lest I too be ill before I achieved my spiritual goal. Equally I felt a need to give more attention to developing a closer union with Baba so when I was confronted with the hardships of ageing, or any other challenge of living, I would be able to rise above the body and be only with Him. Never have I felt so impelled to practice Swami's advice.

My father died on March 1, 1988 and Roberts mother died on March 11, just ten days apart. Our grieving was intensified because of their death so close together.

Sai says, *"Death is not a deplorable event; it is the journey's end; the owner getting out of the car when time*

77

has run out and the goal is reached. It is the consummation, a happy conclusion, which it ought to be if only all are wise enough to treat it as such and be prepared for it." Sathya Sai Newsletter, p. 11

We just finished one funeral and had to prepare for another one. Even though we mourned, I repeated to myself over and over, be calm, stay centered and give love to all! I knew that Sai was carrying and caring for each of us as we mourned the loss of our beloved parents.

The next task was the awesome job of cleaning, selling and disposing of their personal items. Sai says, *"In worldly matters man is misled by the belief that he is the owner of various kinds of properties like houses, lands, vehicles etc. You build a house and call it yours. When you sell it, it is no longer yours. Likewise, you buy a car and call it yours. When it is sold, it ceases to be yours. So, things are yours only as long as you own and use them. Forgetting that all these possessions are temporary like fleeting clouds, you develop undue attachments for them."* Indian Culture and Spirituality p. 19

I was so grateful that we had sold Robert's mother's house two years before because she was a "saver!" Their home had three floors, the main living area, attic, and basement filled to capacity with junk, all of it was memories to mom. She kept everything. Bits of string, aluminum pans that were used when you purchased food that was ready-prepared. Instead of throwing out these wrappings; she kept them. Robert and I spent eight man hours cleaning and filled 16 garbage bags just from one room! It took both sons and wives three months of summer, every week-end to prepare her home for sale.

"You have to do your duty by your kith and kin. But while thus discharging your duties, you should never deviate from the spiritual path. Your secular life should be harmonized with your spiritual life. So long as you live in the world, you have to conform to the rules and regulations governing the worldly affairs. But whatever you may do, you must not lose sight of the Supreme spiritual goal of life. You should recognize the fact that nothing belongs to you whether mother, father, brother, kinsmen, wealth, house etc. All these ephemeral things are related to the changing body which is the basis for all mental aberrations." Indian Culture and Spirituality p. 21

My mom wanted to move to an apartment retirement home which gave her the privacy of her own home but services of the retirement facility. She could eat all her meals in the dining room or prepare them for herself in her own kitchen. Transportation to doctors, grocery stores etc., and social activities were also provided. Her sister-in-law who lived next door to my mom was also recently widowed and moving to the same retirement center. They were support for each other.

Baba's words of *"travel with less luggage"* made a great impression on me. When it is my time to leave a house, I want to get rid of everything that I do not need. It's far better to allow someone else the use of our possessions than to store them for an entire lifetime. What a waste of energy. We are truly possessed by our possessions. The more we own, the more time it takes to care for them and the less time we have to help others. This picturesque learning experience will remain with me forever.

Sai says, *"Nobody brings with him even a tiny piece of cloth at the time of birth, and nobody leaves his address even, at the time of death. If they are really yours, why won't they give you their address at the time of final departure? Nothing belongs to you. Forgetting your own reality and mistaking the unreal as the real in this illusory world, you are creating problems for yourself."*

Indian Culture and Spirituality p. 20

VISIT ALONE

Robert and I have been married for 38 years. How or where does anyone begin to detach from a historic record of 38 years of being together? Not to mention how many lives our souls have shared together!

When I started on this spiritual quest looking for unconditional love it was for the purpose of healing our marriage. Neither one of us really knew the true meaning of love but I was willing to fight for myself and him in the beginning. By this I mean Robert dragged his feet, Swami pushed me, and I pulled Robert.

I never at the time of my commitment would have conceived of the idea of detachment. We were so far apart in our relationship that my only concept of marriage was union. I wanted to unite our relationship with the bond of love..... never ever realizing that we would eventually learn to detach our united relationship

81

for a higher union with our Divine Spark, the God within.

We have engaged ourselves since 1968, 23 years, in the role of learning to love one another through the tools of self-analysis, knowledge, correction, practice and eventual change of behavior. This involved hours of communication. All this effort, along with a huge investment of time and energy bound us closer and closer together.

It was our belief that God was love. It was also a fact that we were not treating each other with the love that Jesus taught. "Love one another as you love yourself." Instead we were enveloped with selfishness. So our task at hand was to learn selflessness.

Sai said, *"Love is God, God is love. Where there is love, there God is certainly evident. Love more and more people, love them more and more intensely. Transform the love into service, transform the service into worship. That is the highest spiritual practice"*. Sathya Sai Speaks 4, p. 309

Now this is easier to do with friends and neighbors because of our self-image. Controlling the negative behavior within our own household is the **real** challenge! Why? Because the most natural place to air our feelings of discontent is within the walls of our home. We show selfishness through our words and actions. Our patience, sweet words, and kind actions are easier to give outside the family unit. Our home life is where our inside image, meaning what we really feel or think, is more openly expressed.

I have thought many times of the great wisdom of God giving us two images, an inside and outside one. He has made our outside image, meaning how we want others to see us, seem more important because of the rewards we can receive from society such as jobs, promotions, friendship, marriage, honors, wealth, fame, etc... Because of this we will strive harder to control our negative thoughts, words and actions. Perhaps if we did not have an outside image, we would have mistreated mankind even more severely than history shows.

On the other hand, if we did not have the escape valve, of letting some of the pressure and stress of living escape from within us through the hallways of our homelife, we could end up with destructive anxiety and anger. I am definitely not saying that these two types of release and control are absolute. We step over the boundaries many times but usually these inner and outer identities, help us to modify our behavior.

God gives us these boundaries for self-expression to help us learn self-control. That is the whole object of spirituality: to gain knowledge about our true self and control over our senses.

Sai says, *"You should resort to the path of inquiry and thereby develop the firm conviction, I am neither the body nor the sense organs. I am the ever-blissful Atma. Only when you are unshakably established in this conviction, will the sense organs cease to trouble you."* Indian Culture and Spirituality, p. 58

Only when this is achieved can we serve others with un-conditional love.

Sai says, *"Recognize the truth that the body is given to man to perform selfless service. Selfless service reveals the*

Divinity within man." Divine Discourse November 19, 1990

This was the objective, goal and motive God had to teach us before we could change our selfish love into selfless love. Never was there a hint of detachment from one another... we were striving for unity and harmony with each other. We had concentrated all our energy on developing a positive home life. Before we included the entire creation as our family we had first to learn to give within our own family unit. This is the place that God uses as our laboratory to teach us, by trial and error, about our reactions, and the nature of our family chemistry, and the effects of negative and positive thoughts, words, and actions.

But Sai Baba has taught us that the path to God expands even more. It expands beyond our relationships with husband, wife and children. It expands beyond our desires for material sensation. It expands beyond the world of ego power and recognition. Love expands to the inclusion of all and exclusion of self.

When Swami remarried us in 1983, it was a spiritual marriage. Since then He has been prompting us to think differently about our relationship. He has given little hints by saying, *"Don't touch"* when Robert touched me and said *"husband or has been husband"* to me.

Now that our children are grown and we are not active householders, He is asking us to detach mentally from the role of husband and wife; not physically. We are to think of God as our marriage partner. We have enormous programming in the opposite direction. But this is His responsibility; I haven't a clue where to begin.

84

After both parents' funerals had settled, Swami told me in meditation, "Come this summer for a two month visit, alone without Robert." A cold shiver went through my body. I have never been separated from Robert for two months, nor traveled to a foreign country, alone. What a test and a fear for me to tackle. Needless to say I was a little apprehensive in telling Robert this new message.

As always He received it well. He had no doubt that the message was real, and not conjured up by some fantasy of mine. In fact, he thought it would be very good for us and a great opportunity for our own personal growth.

I have seen women traveling alone to see Sai Baba many times. They feel extremely protected by Baba so I too knew through my previous experiences with Sai that He would never leave my side.

Robert and I decided that I would go to India in August and September. We wanted to spend some time this summer using our condo on the lake. Our life had been so hectic since we arrived home and we just wanted some of the solitude that the lakeside living provided.

The next day Sai Baba changed the departure time. He said, "Come directly after the Mid-West Regional Conference, stay June and July." Our Lord Sai is determined to poke at every desire! I fully accepted going to India in August and September, now He switched the months to June and July. This change confronted me with two desires and created confusion within my mind as to what Sai was telling me and what my desires were telling me... June & July or August & September?????

It was May 25, when Swami told me to sit down and write. He gave me this message. "Are you prepared to listen to my words now?" Yes, I replied. He continued to speak to me inside as I wrote down His message.

"Why do you fight or resist my will? You must succumb anyway..... **I will always get you.** I asked you to come in June and July! You wanted to come in August and September because you didn't want to leave your mother since she recently lost her husband. You didn't want to leave Robert and the lake house because you would miss most of the summer at the lake. So your desires, not I, talked yourself into August. If you stay home till August, the waiting will prove to be more difficult.

"Don't resist, come, I will clear the path so the journey in June is possible. I will accept either time from you for this trip but I would prefer June. I want you to get in the habit of accepting my first request regardless of the inconvenience, to your desires."

I obeyed. I was on the airline's waitlist for June 1 departure to India. He did clear the path and my ticket soon became confirmed. August proved to be the month that Sai slipped in the shower and injured His hip, and there was less darshan.

The Regional Conference is always the last week-end in May, on Memorial Day. It is scheduled then because of the extra holiday on Monday. Robert and I have served as committee members since the Conference of 1978.

I knew the benefits that we derive from Sai Conferences. His energy multiplies with our increased devotion and love. The devotees become living channels of His Prema. I knew Swami was sending me to India with extra love energy.

I was met by our taxi driver, Bala Gopal. I heaved a sigh of relief.... because I knew I was nearly home. I spent the night in the hotel and was going to rest one day and travel to Prasanthi the next.

But I had an unexpected reaction. It was the first time since I left Robert that I was isolated and alone. I was overcome with the loss of his companionship. I missed him so much; I was extremely shaken. I didn't know what to do. I needed to distract my feelings and thoughts but the solitude of the hotel room didn't help.

Sai Baba tells the story, *"There is a girl in one house. There is a young man in another house. Their houses are almost side by side. But the girl does not know anything about the young man, and the young man does not know anything about the girl living in the neighboring house. One day, the girl fell seriously ill. That day all the people in the house were hectic and several doctors were called in. When the boy in the neighboring house heard the noise, he thought it was a disturbance to his studies, and, therefore, he closed his window and started reading. But in course of time, as a result of destiny, this boy got married to that girl in the neighboring house. The marriage took place in the morning. In the afternoon the girl developed a stomach ache and the bridegoom felt very anxious for the girl and her stomach ache. Where and when did he develop this attachment to the girl? Because he got married to her, even a little stomach ache upset him. When the same girl fell dangerously ill some time ago, he did not feel even the slightest anxiety for her because at that time there was no attachment or relationship with that girl. So, affection and attachment, are responsible for all joys and sorrows. We must try to attain that serene state of mind, that equanimity which enables you not to be elated by joy or depressed by sorrow. When you are able to attain that equanimity of mind, then you can attain Samadhi."* Summer Showers 1972, p. 240 & 241

I went downstairs to talk with Gopal. I was deeply thankful for his immediate perception. He said, "Madam, you need to go today to Prasanthi, not tomorrow. When you see Baba, you will feel good. I will arrange a taxi for you."

How happy I was for his solution and he was indeed correct. As soon as I was underway, the pressure I felt of Robert's absence, disappeared. How happy I was to see the Prasanthi gate!

I was not prepared for the beautiful welcoming surprise that Swami had in store for me. I was wondering as I walked up the flights of stairs if Ginny and Bob Reinhardt were home. When I knocked on their door, a response from inside said, "They are in 4-D." 'Great,' I thought, 'that is my apartment!'

As I knocked and entered they welcomed me with open arms. My my entire apartment was completely redone. It was magnificent! Not only re-done but all set-up. Our apartment was transformed into a work of art according to the village standard. Bob made sure that the workmanship was the best available. I could not believe the transformation. I could only feel the hours he labored in love on our room, and the support and sacrifice made by his wife, Ginny. When the husband is gone; the wife has more work to do. We shall be eternally grateful to them both.

I had wondered how I would manage moving the furniture from the locked kitchen - but now I discovered that every detail of cleaning, readiness and preparation of the apartment was already completed. I wanted to cry because of the sweetness of Sai. He took care of every single detail through the loving hearts of the Reinhardts.

Sai says, *"Wisdom can dawn only when a devotee's thoughts, words, and deeds are dedicated to God. God loves those who love their fellow beings. So, one has to install God in the heart and undertake the task of fulfilling the duties He has laid down for them. This is the lesson that true education instills."* Sathya Sai Newsletter Summer 1993, p. 11

In my first darshan I got the second row, Swami came near saying, "Maya, Maya, Maya," as He motioned for a woman nearby to go for an interview. I remembered His words, noted them in my diary because often the first days events give the theme or emphasis for each trip. Maya means illusion......

For the first several days of darshan, Swami gave me first and second row seats. Several times He looked directly to me, and one morning as He looked I said, "The book..." He answered, a gentle *"wait, wait."* Well now I

89

have the second word to His message. Maya and wait, wait. Neither word thrilled me.

I had rewritten some of the manuscript since my last trip. Did His reply mean that I needed to do more work on the book or was He implying that He would accept it this trip but I must wait for when He calls me? Anyway.... He did give me some direction and recognized that I did have a book.

In my early morning meditation, Swami said, "You do not need to grab in the sand, grabbing for my feet. I will give them to you at the appropriate time. To touch the physical form is not nearly as important as touching the heart of God through obedience and devotion. Sit in the arches or on a chair."

Our Lord knew that I was asking for padnamaskar and He also knew the condition of my back. I have neck, middle and lower back trouble. He was instructing me to be sensible and more comfortable. His message was the same on my last trip. "Sit on the chairs, I will call you when I need you."

I heard Swami say within, "Touch the Heart of God with your devotion and obedience instead of touching His feet in darshan." This message expanded my awareness and clearly instructed me. I must obey Him and returned to sitting in the back. I thought, "The Lord appears to be fickle. Sometimes He seems to **adore** me; other times He simply **ignores** me!" I felt so distant from Robert and I missed his companionship. Now Swami was also putting me on the back burner. All I was receiving from Him was "Back Darshan" a view of only His back. I felt ignored.

Baba tells us, *"Be humble and loving, wherever you are, in whatever company. Remember the Names of the Lord, indicating His Glory, His Mercy, His Love. Then, all egoistic feelings will flee from you. Life is a game of football. You are the ball, and you are bound to be thrown and kicked about this side and that. How long have you to bear this treatment? Until the air is fully out of the ball. Deflate it, no one will kick it again. The air that inflates it is the ego! When the ego is out, Bliss comes in."* Thought For The Day, November 19, 1991

I stayed mostly to myself and I lived alone. My dear friend Catherine who I had counted on for some companionship gave me a note shortly after I arrived. "I cannot talk now; maybe in a month." So He was cutting me off from all outside communication.

I was used to being alone during the day but always had some interaction when Robert came home. This I missed. No one to share the everyday events with except Him, the Divine partner inside. This trip had the clear markings of an "inner trip."

I spent my spare time writing. I wrote another article for Sanathana Sarathi on "Sai Vision vs. Television". In fact I focused on children and the Bal Vikas Programs during this trip. I wrote questions to Sai Baba in my diary on better methods of instructing and disciplining children in the Sai Family Programs. This was clearly my time for quiet contemplation and renewal of inner contact with God.

Every time I went to the lines and took a chit, I would get very high numbers and only see Swami's back during darshan. This trip was certainly enforcing the same behavior modification as the last trip. Swami is a master!

I could hear His voice within so clearly this time. And He was always helping me to understand His point of view. One day He said, "Your reality is a fantasy. This entire world is a fantasy. Rita, you are fantasizing, a fantasy. You are clutching on to what you think is real; not what is real. It is not necessary to have this physical form; it is only necessary to be with **God's** internal form."

I was expecting Audrey Staton, a devotee from St. Louis who was going to spend the final six weeks with me. On July 11, my sister and another new devotee would also be joining us.

I was so happy to see Audrey. I had successfully stayed alone for these last 10 days. I had definitely planned on Audrey bringing a letter from Robert. I asked Audrey, "Do you have a letter from Robert for me?" "No," she replied. I continued, "Did he give you a message?" "No." "Did he phone before you left?" "No," she replied. "I thought maybe he would call but I didn't hear from him," she answered. I was so disappointed.

Three weeks had passed and still no word from Robert. I had been writing frequently. I couldn't imagine why he had not written.

The pressure of being denied any attention from Sai Baba and receiving no communication from Robert came to a head. I wrote two letters one to Sai Baba and the other one to Robert. It was good therapy, I released my feelings. The essence of the letters stated that "I don't want either of you for my husband." I even told Robert that I had his charge cards and on my way home, I would stop in Hong Kong, shop and charge it to him. I'd spend his retirement money. I felt hurt, neglected and angry.

*"What exactly is the cause of all grief? It is the attachment to the body that produces grief as well as its immediate precursors; affection and hate. These two are the results of the intellect considering some things and conditions as beneficial, and some other things and conditions as not. This is a delusion, this idea of beneficence and malevolence. Still you get attached to objects that are considered beneficial and you start hating the others. But, from the highest point of view, there is neither. The distinction is just meaningless. There is no two at all. How can there be good and bad then? To see two where there is only one, that is delusion or ignorance. The ignorance that plunged Arjuna into grief was of this nature seeing many when there is only **ONE**.* Sanathana Sarathi July 1992 p. 158

I put Swami's letter on the altar and mailed Robert's. Several nights later, I awoke from sleep. Swami told me, "Bring the letter to me in darshan." I replied, "Oh no, Swami, I couldn't give that letter to you in person." "Why not?" He replied. "Because I wrote it while I was angry and hurt," I said. He continued, "But I am your Mother and Father, who else can you complain to but the God within. I want to share in all your joy and sorrow. Bring the letter to me in darshan tomorrow and I will give you a front row place and padnamaskar."

My ears perked up. "Padnamaskar", I said. "Padnamaskar", He replied. Swami had said the "magic word." That got me. I would do anything to get that close and kiss His feet. I took the letter and headed for the chit line the following morning.

I was so excited because my row was number two. I just barely got a first row seat. It was on the side but Swami would be able to give me His feet from here. I waited and tried to prepare myself spiritually for the act of surrender to His Divine Lotus Feet.

Swami walked towards me and I held my breath in expectation. "Oh, just a little farther, my Lord", I coached inside. His eyes met mine. He took my letter and as I bent to His Feet, He said, *"Very, very, happy."* I was overcome with relief, gratitude and joy.

The anxiety that had followed me for days became calm and silent. I savored the moment and memory. I felt so relieved. It had been a long three years of daily struggle since I had last heard those words. I would have traveled any distance, anywhere, anytime to hear His voice say *"Very, happy."*

He was telling me that He was pleased with me, even though I had felt so badly before this darshan. I was extremely grateful. This was the climax of my trip.

Some days later Audrey was called in for an interview. I knew that I was not to go unless sent for. I must confess that almost every person I knew at Prasanthi received an interview during my stay but.... me.

My youngest sister, Judy arrived with Andrea. Now

the foursome was complete. Judy had a letter. And it seems that Robert laughed and laughed at my angry letter. He called our son Craig and said, "Mom must have really been mad, Craig. Listen to what she wrote." After reading the letter to his son he asked, "Why hasn't mom received the letters I sent with your friend?"

I received immense pleasure having my sister come for her first visit. She had been a devotee as long as I. Now she had the opportunity to visit Baba. Judy and Andrea wanted an interview. Their words sounded familiar. For these two ladies, I prayed for their wish to come true.

We were blessed with tremendous physical comfort. Food supplies flowed into our room. There was an abundance of supplies at all time, and we were even given a harmonium. This was definitely grace for Judy, who loved music. She could sing, play the guitar and piano, she wrote English devotional songs, and conducted children and adult choirs. Music was her one great love and it brought her much joy, so I knew this to be a sweet touch of His grace. Almost every evening, we would sing. It soothed the heart ache, we each carried. Judy, Audrey and Andrea had excellent voices and together the four of us would sing praise and worship songs in harmony.

We spent three weeks together, doing the chores, going to darshan, sharing and supporting each other. It was an unusual experience for me. I had not had female companionship like this since I was in high school. Sometimes we would giggle ourselves to sleep. All of us commonly shared family responsibilities. So we all felt a sense of freedom and had high expectations at the beginning, but as the days dwindled the high hopes of wanting an interview slid into the low !

Walking a tight rope is easier when there is only one artist on the wire. Balancing four on the same rope is another story, especially when Swami is the director and owns the circus.

Our trip was to be concluded on Gurupoornima. After Swami repeatedly ignored my sister, Judy, for three weeks, she questioned Baba as her appropriate guru. She thought maybe He wanted her to identify only with Jesus.

She wrote a note asking Sai Baba to take it if He wanted her as His devotee. This culminated the night before Gurupoornima, naturally......

Judy went to darshan with note in hand. She had an excellent seat at the end of a path that Sai Baba would have to take. Judy was guaranteed a walk past but only He knew if the note would be taken.

With all His Glory and Majesty, Swami took her note! Judy was so happy, and so were we! Swami can turn our pain into joy in an instant. Swami selected the most perfect day to convey His message to her. How did He know that the question that plagued her most was, "Did He want her for His devotee?" And what better time for his answer to be manifested than on Gurupoornima? The question, the time, the place, the date, and the woman all came together.

Before we packed to leave, Swami explained to me,

within, why I was ignored by Him. He said, "Rita, you have come to India leaving your earthly husband home. You had intended to substitute Robert's physical attention with mine, and you expected me to give you that attention.

"I'm not detaching you from Robert and replacing it with my form. Why would I want to replace one attachment for another? You must understand that my form is also temporary. I don't **encourage** attachments; it is my job to **discourage** them. **I don't encourage desire; I destroy it!"**

An added "Leela" concerning the letters that Robert wrote which I never received. The letters were given to a friend of Craig's whose father, a foreign director, was going to India. I discovered this information two days before I returned to the U.S. I went to see the father and all he remembered were the letters his son gave to him from devotee's for Sai Baba. He gave all the letters to Sai Baba over a month ago. He told me that when Swami receives letters for someone else, He gives them to Mr. Katumba Rao. I should check with him. I found out that he had received no letters from Baba for me.

It was now very clear that Sai Baba withheld my letters from home. He wanted me to realize my attachments. The absence of communication from Robert, intensified my experience hence the layers of my attachments rose to my consciousness.

The second words I heard from Sai were *"wait, wait."* The book was again shelved for this trip. I went home to re-write.

I had conquered some of my fears and managed with God's grace to be absent from Robert for two months. Also, I experienced life again at Puttaparthi with no interview and dealt with some of my fear. I received greater inner communication and practiced adjusting to very little outside contact with the form. His Omnipresence had overseen every detail of my trip. It was a "biggy " and I was glad to be going home.

As I departed I heard Him say, "The closer you become to me; the closer you become me."

Robert and the children welcomed me with bunches of love. My husband had strung computer banners throughout the house expressing His love and joy at my return. We were aware that our love had grown deeper and stronger.

Two weeks after I had arrived home the excitement of my return had worn off and I began feeling depressed. I had taken two trips now to see Sai Baba and had had virtually no attention from His Divine form, and it had been five years since my last interview. On all our previous trips Swami had spoiled us with His love and attention. Now that was gone. I had been addicted to pop, sugar, coffee and tea but removing them did not create this severe pain of emptiness in my emotional heart. I began to realize that what I was feeling was "withdrawal symptoms." I had become addicted to His Sweetness that flows from His form. If only I could hear Him speak to me, smile, pat my head, kiss His feet, hold His hand or have His eyes meet mine. I ached inside, and the uncertainty of no future attention made me feel even worse. Devotees from the ashram would tell me that I had reached a new level and I would only have contact inside. I cried out, Swami Dear, how can I adjust to this?

I sat down to write a letter to Swami and my inner Sai Voice began talking. "You feel that you have traveled a great distance to see Sai Baba and because of no physical attention you feel empty. Is it because My love only extends to the interview room? If God's Love only fell on those who entered the interview room, God's Love would be limited. My Love is without bounds. It flows through and is within everything.

"All those who sit at My feet whether in My interview room, the darshan compound or before Me anywhere in the world, are with Me and I with them, every moment to moment.

"My Love is the life force that makes you see, speak, hear and feel. It is the God within, it is He I want you to find, not this Physical Form that is being symbolized in Sathya Sai Baba.

"Do you think because My eyes have not set upon yours that I am not aware of your Presence? For me to avoid you or anyone it takes greater conscious awareness. How can I avoid you unless I am aware of your presence?

"Since I gave you little outward recognition you feel **demoted** instead of **promoted**. But you are now stronger and no longer need constant outward attention. You have been **promoted** to sitting in the wings of the Lord, always ready and waiting to Serve Him when He calls.

"Do you think I was unaware of your broken heart, sitting behind a large pillar so far removed from My physical form on your very last darshan? I feel every pain and joy experienced by man. I am always there within you. I know how gallant you fought to hold back the tears of grief and disappointment, and that is why My Grace rescued you and lifted you above those emotions.

"This trip to Baba was a test of Surrender....a test of surrendering to MY WILL. Do you remember before you came how you said to Robert, "If I get an interview with Swami I will ask Him what does He want to tell me - not ask what I want to know?"

"This entire trip was exactly My answer to that question. I gave you what I WANTED; not what you wanted. My actions conveyed My message. "Surrender everything to Me and I will provide and care for your every need. Recall your trip and you will see that more than needs were provided for thee!"

RETIREMENT

In my twenties and thirties, the word Retirement was just a word in the dictionary but meant nothing to me. Sometime in my early forties the word began taking on some identity for me. We were saving and investing money for our retirement. When I approached fifty, the word actuated from the dusty book shelf and began to define a possible lifestyle for our future. It seemed like the reality of being a senior citizen soon, finally was born in my consciousness. I muttered the same words that all humans ultimately speak, "Where did the time go? How did I get so old? I still feel as young as I did years ago?"

In December 1988, my son Craig and wife, Patricia went to spend Christmas with Sai Baba. Before Craig departed, Robert asked Craig to ask Swami, "If we could come the following September for a visit?" Robert was nearing 55 years and wanted to see Baba and ask if he could retire early and spend the rest of our lives serving Him.

101

Robert's employer recently removed the remaining obstacle "Health Insurance", and made it possible for us to consider early retirement. With the new retirement plan, full retirement benefits were reduced from 60 years to 55 years. This included full medical coverage for both of us.

When Craig returned home he surprised us. Instead of having asked permission for us to come, he had written a note saying, "Swami, should my father retire from his current job at age 55 in 1990? Please give me a verbal reply. Love Craig." As Swami approached Craig, he held the note open, written in large letters for Swami to read immediately. Baba replied, *"Yes, I will take care of him."*

'WOW,' we thought, there was our answer! Swami said, *"Yes."* We were overjoyed because it meant we could spend more time with Swami in India. It was a dream come true.

This happened 9 months sooner than we expected, the Master had taken us again by surprise. This meant that we would soon be free from the householders' duties. A light at the end of the tunnel. It almost seemed make-believe, after 34 years of living a certain lifestyle and now a change, but we were absolutely ready for something different!

Swami removed all the doubt, worry and confusion because He told us directly. It was a very **BIG** decision to make without Sai's specific word. By instructing Craig, He made it possible for us to have an easier transition.

I'll never forget several years ago, when Joan asked us to bring a picture of Tony with us to India and ask Sai

Baba if he was a good husband for her. They had known each other since high school. I was taken completely by surprise because Joan had no interest in Sai Baba. I wondered if this decision was based on Sai Baba choosing Craig's marriage partner. I was pleased that she asked.

When Robert was in the darshan line he held out Tony's picture, for Swami's Blessing. As Swami walked by He said to Robert, *"Italian."* After darshan, Robert was puzzled. He told me what had happened. Robert asked me, "Why did Swami say Italian, when Tony is American? I replied, "He is American, but his parents are Italian, so he is Italian American!" Robert laughed, Swami certainly caught Robert off-guard, and I'm certain that Baba loved every minute of it.

In the interview room, Robert gave Tony's picture to Sai Baba, and asked, "Will this young man be a good husband for my daughter?" Sai replied, *"Good friends for a long time."* Robert repeated, as any anxious father would who wants the best for their daughters, "Will he be a good husband?" *"Yes,"* answered Sai, *"He is a good boy, he will be prosperous and a good husband."*

His timing again seemed to be Omni-Perfect. Joan announced that she would be getting married in October 1989, a few months before Robert retired in April 1990. We would soon be through the role of parenting, Swami was tying the knots, removing the loose ends of our karma.

There is an interesting story on how Swami helped us in a sensitive situation with the wedding preparations. Only because of His teachings and grace was I able to confront an uncomfortable problem..... Robert and I had gone to the lake for the week-end and when we arrived home on Sunday night, I asked, Joan, "Did you and your bridesmaids find dresses on Saturday? "Yes, mom and they are so perfect. The girls tried on every dress in St. Louis (she mentioned all the stores) and there was always something unflattering about the dresses for at least one of the girls. Except for this dress, it looks good on all five bridesmaids. "Really, I said?" I thought, what is she leading up to?

"Did you get emerald green?" (the color she wanted) No, this dress didn't come in that color. It's the newest and most fashionable color this year, it's in all the Bridal books!" "Well... tell me," I said. "They are black satin," replied Joan. "Black for a wedding?" I inquired. "Joan, that's not an appropriate color." She replied, "Well, mom perhaps not in your day, but it's a rage in today's fashion.

Our children are products of the age of communication and they are masters at convincing parents that the old moral virtues and values don't apply to the 1990's because they are obsolete and out-dated. But Sai Baba has taught me that spiritual Truths prevail forever. It does not change from age to age. Kindness, respect, honor to parents etc., remain the same and don't change their meaning with each new generation. Now that I know this, my children can no longer convince me that I'm old-fashioned or in error. I have the weapon of Sai Baba's Wisdom in my hands.

She continued her well prepared case. "One of the

greatest advantages of this dress is that since they are a sheath style and strapless, the girls can wear them for parties, after the wedding. You know, mom, bridesmaids' dresses are so expensive and they didn't mind the cost since they can use them again."

"What do you think about strapless dresses for a church wedding, Joan?" I asked. I was trying to get her to think about it. She replied, "Mary Ann's bridesmaid dresses are strapless and she's getting married in church." 'Oh great,' I'm thinking, Mary Ann was her best girlfriend. No matter what I said now, I would be offending Joan or Mary Ann. But I was still hopeful, thinking, that next week they could look again, but this ray of hope was quickly ended. Joan said, "The dresses are ordered and everyone put money down, as deposit." "But Joan," I asked, "Why didn't you consult with me before you made this final decision?" She answered, "This is my wedding, Mother." I said, "This is our wedding Joan. Dad and I are the hosts for this occasion."

Inside, I'm calling on Swami, for help. This conversation has all the trappings for an argument. So I ended our talk by saying, "I'll have to think about it, we'll talk later," and I went to my room.

Sai Baba has taught me so much. The old Rita, before Baba, would have wanted to settle this problem immediately, even though it was not a good time. The conversation would have ended in an argument.

Three teachings of Baba prevented my old behavior and helped me to have some control. 1. Baba says, *"Speech is so powerful, slip while walking, the injury can be repaired; but slip while talking, the injury is irreparable."* 2. *"Five minutes of anger damages the relationship for five generations."* SSS I, p. 87

Joan's conversation is a good example of "parent pressure." Children are confronted with peer pressure but we are confronted with parent pressure. I mean, children trying to convince us to use their conscience instead of ours. I was caught in a no-win situation. If I had disagreed, I would have insulted her best friend, rejected their judgment in selecting bridal gowns, cost her girlfriends more expense, time and energy, limited them to select gowns at this store because of their down payment, embarrassed Joan, and made her wedding unfashionable..... that's parent pressure! You almost need to be a defense lawyer to raise children today because of their smartness.

So I called Sai Baba, asking for His legal help, and gave myself some quiet time to prepare my case and talk with my husband when he got home. Several days later Joan and I had our talk.

I said, "Joan, I want to share with you, dad's and my thoughts about the bridesmaids' dresses. Marriage to us is a sacred institution given to man from God. In the spiritual realm, white and black are symbolic of good and evil forces, virtue vs. vice. The bride has dressed traditionally in white because it is symbolic of purity, virginity, and morality. We believe that the color black is not in accordance with the sacredness of marriage. If black is now being used in wedding ceremonies, it is an indication that evil, has crept into our marriage system and is even invading the very day that should represent all that is good and noble in the unity of man and woman.

"Let me stress the importance of this day for Tony and you. The commitment to love and serve God and each other is forever. This decision will affect your entire life. The wedding itself is an example, a statement to those who view it of the sacredness in which your vows are being made. This wedding ceremony will live one hundred years from now and be remembered and seen in the photos by your children and grandchildren.

"Sai Baba tells us, *Modesty is essential for women; it is her priceless jewel.*" I believe that strapless dresses are not an expression of the virtues in women; they inflame sexuality. We are trying to kindle in our guests the thoughts of purity, femininity and modesty; not a cocktail party atmosphere. Each married person in attendance will reflect back to their own wedding day and review their relationship now and then. Let us help them to remember that marriage is not a 'swinging affair,' but a permanent commitment to love and sacrifice.

"God would be very displeased with your father and I if we allowed these dresses. We are held responsible to God for the behavior of our children while in our home. Please tell your girlfriends our views, and that I'm sorry for the inconvenience. God will take care of the rest..... "

I promised Joan that I would go with her to the store and explain to the manager my view on the dresses and see if she would release them from their contract and refund the girls' money. Joan was embarrassed as I spoke but the woman understood and returned the money. We were both very happy.

The girls found beautiful emerald green dresses with hats to match. His amazing grace worked this small miracle for us. How often He says, *"If you take one step towards Me; I'll take 10 towards you."* But to take that step requires time and energy. It is much easier to let these mistakes go instead of correcting them. And to increase the degree of difficulty, time is most scarce because of our lifestyle.

Throughout the entire wedding day, His Love was shown by the perfection and beauty of the ceremony. His Love was felt by the people who expressed their feelings of joy, happiness, and pleasure to attend the wedding of Tony and Joan.

It is always alluring to watch Sai playfully capture the heart of someone who is not interested. Joan when she was very young and her childhood friends made fun of our Sai Baba pictures and she grew-up with these embarrassing childhood memories. Even as an adult she carried the same stigma. Whenever her friends came to our home she would remove any photos, no matter how small, to avoid any possible embarrassment.

This scenario had gone on till one summer while during her holiday from college. She worked as a tour guide,and one of the girls who worked with her went to New York. When she came back, she showed Joan her photos.

That evening when she came home, she rushed to me excited, "Mom, you're never going to believe who's in this picture!" As she showed it to me she said, "What do you see, mom, what do you see?" I replied, "Oh, there's a picture of Sai Baba." "But guess where it is, mom?" replied Joan. Her girlfriend had visited the Hard Rock Cafe in New York and took some pictures, not knowing anything about Sai Baba. It was Swami's joke for Joan! There Sai was as big as life on a public wall where her peers visited, with His motto next to it, *"Love All; Serve All."* Swami certainly got her attention and hinted to her to look at the childhood humiliation with the eyes and wisdom of her present maturity. My sweet Joan stopped hiding pictures.

The one and a half years before we retired were extremely heartbreaking for me. When I arrived home from my visit to Baba, Donna, Tara, and boyfriend were waiting for me. They had come to St. Louis a few days before I arrived home and Robert was waiting for me to make a decision. They wanted us to give them a home etc... again... for the third time.

What a heavy judgment to make. We couldn't provide for them again because it would not last, and we could not bring Donna and Tara home because the boyfriend was still with her. There was nothing we could do, they had to want to build a life together for their child. How hurtful it was to stand by and watch.

How many times has Our Dear Swami had to stand by and watch me making dreadful mistakes. But if He didn't allow me to make them, would I ever have learned that it was a mistake? Tough Love is allowing the person to pick-up their own pieces in life, as we become supportive watchers instead of doers. Self-esteem or self-confidence does not become our own when someone else does it for us. In fact it can have the reverse effect and reduce self-esteem.

So we watched as they moved into an inner city shelter. I devoted most of my time to helping her learn how to care for herself and her new daughter. We were especially concerned about the welfare of this new child but Sai was always there to remind me that it is His child, not mine and He is the one providing and protecting them. He explicitly showed me His Omnipotent protection one night that I will never forget.

After months of living in the shelter, they moved to a housing project. One night Robert and I were going to their apartment for a visit. When we arrived, we found Donna very upset and Tara crying. She said, "When she unlocked her door, a man came from behind and pushed her into the apartment. The boyfriend was not at home. The crazy man, went into the kitchen, got the butcher knife and told her that he would molest her and kill them both." Donna started screaming and pounding on the wall of her neighbor. Her action frightened the intruder and he ran. We arrived just in time to help her through this tragedy. Donna was very courageous and brave.

Swami is always saying that he does not normally interfere with our karma but softens it with grace. The grace in this case was saving our children's lives and allowing us to arrive immediately afterwards to help them over the shock under the protecting umbrella of His love. Oh, how thankful we are to Sai.

We called the police, filed a report and listened to the advice given to us by the officer. He told us that this housing project was the worst in St. Louis, and no place for Donna and Tara to be safe.

We moved them the next day, and again they were blessed with an apartment, car, and jobs through the grace of Sai. It lasted a few months and again Donna's boyfriend left with another woman. I felt like I was riding an emotional roller coaster watching Donna going over and over the same track and wondering when and how she would ever get off? I wondered how she could stand it. Her agony was great but I could not help her to understand that if she left this boyfriend, the father of Tara, she could come home and we would help her. The knot in the karmic tie that bound them together seemed to get more and more tangled instead of loosening. We were so disappointed for her, and our hopes were smashed again.

It seemed that Swami was burning off my karma before we retired. And as each day passed, the word retirement glistened like the pot of gold at the end of the rainbow. Many days it helped my sanity because I could see a temporary end to this nightmare. The word that held no meaning for me most of my life now grew into a treasure chest of hope. It was an intense time and many days I thought my heart would break, especially watching the lifestyle they had. Thank God, I had Sai Baba or I would never have been able to watch with love and help when needed.

Swami says, *"Listen to Me. When you wake up, feel that*

you are entering the stage to play the role assigned to you by the Lord; pray that you may act it well and earn His approbation. At night, when you retire to sleep, feel that you are entering the green-room after the scene, but with the dress of your role on; for perhaps the role is not yet over and you have not yet been permitted to take the dress off. Perhaps you have to make another entrance the next morning. Do not worry about that. Place yourself fully at His disposal; He knows. He has written the Play and He knows how it will end and how it will go on. Yours is but to act and retire." Thought For The Day, December 10, 1991.

In His worldly laboratory of experience, it proved in reality to be a golden opportunity for me to practice surrender in an extremely sensitive area for a woman. It struck at my very core of motherhood. Some days I had minute to minute combat. I'd give it to Him, He threw it back and since I was still attached, I caught it. I'd give it back to Him, and again my mind would take it back. I had a fertile field to practice the act of surrender in a most provocative set of circumstances.

I remember in Kodaikanal 1992, Swami told us, *"Practice is effort made. It is a skill no different than learning to walk, talk, or eat. Spirituality needs to be practiced."*

He also says, *"People today pursue studies all their life, but hardly practice what they have learnt. Practice is more essential than the mere acquisition of knowledge. It is not accumulation of information that is important, but the transformation of oneself. Of what use is all the information you have gathered? How much of it have you put to practical use? How much bliss have you derived from it?*

112

The answer will be: a hero in gathering information; a zero in putting it into practice. In this way, life is being wasted rather than being purposeful." Sanathana Sarathi April 93, p. 88

As the New Year approached, I could only pray that Sai helped to make it a better one for our family. I was exceedingly happy to close this year and welcome in 1990, our year to stay with Sai Baba.

We were now down the final stretch of selling our house, and disposing of most of our worldly possessions. We had the children pick and choose what they wanted. I kept my ear tuned to Sai's inner station. Writing His messages have now became a familiar pattern. It was helpful having a permanent record of His advice. It gave me every opportunity to read repeatedly. His words gave me wisdom, serenity and peace. I was comforted by His Omnipresence. I heard His words speaking in my heart and I wrote:

"Put your hand in Mine, and your trust in Me. Hold my hand and I will show you my kingdom. We have been partners and friends long enough for Trust to be established. You are ready, for this new journey. I am not asking you to do something beyond your abilities.

"You and Robert love to travel. You like to see different places and experience different lifestyles. Well, I am offering you a "Trip of a Lifetime." Instead of traveling in the outer world; you can travel with me in the inner world. I will provide, for all your needs. You are my guest. NOT ONE THING DO YOU BRING, only yourself. Leave all desires at home.

"You have always wanted to travel around the world when you retired. But instead, you will travel through the Inner Universe with God to see His Heavenly Kingdom.

"Intensify your sadhana. Prepare for your trip to see and be with me. Don't waste any time or energy. Time is precious. Keep healthy. You will have to cut ties that bind before you leave. Lighten your load of possessions internal and external.

"I promise you that your quality of life will immensely improve. Your parental responsibilities are over. You will reverse your role. You are MY children and I'm your parents!"

Sai says, *"The joy you experience will be in inverse proportion to your desires. The greater the desires the less the happiness you will experience. Therefore, try constantly to reduce your desires. In the journey of life, as in a railway journey, the less luggage (desires) you carry the greater the comfort you will have."* Sanathana Sarathi April 93, p. 89

We followed Sai's advice, unloaded possessions and desires. We started in the basement. We took our collected treasures of a lifetime each holding a special memory and parted with them. It was an excellent exercise because Swami asked us to lighten our load of internal and external possessions. We found that each item, had a place in our memory. As we went through our stuff, we relived some of the memories of both the happy times and of some not so happy. As we placed the articles in boxes to be given away, this act seemed to help remove the mental and physical attachment. Breaking up our own household, served as a useful spiritual exercise. It also proved to be a good reason to do the job yourself instead of waiting too long when you no longer are capable. We benefited far more than if our children had done it for us.

When we had our household goods down to bare bone, Swami gave us more inner instructions. On February 1990, He said, "Your past was devoted to karmic activities. They were necessary for you to understand the reality of God.

"Where do you proceed? Straight to me, in Puttaparti. Your life has exact timing and planning. I am its ruler, the authority and power in your life. All you must do is show up. Do not concern yourself with the future, I am it's Master. Do not worry, my little mother hen, I will protect your nest and flock in your absence. Your children are mine.

"So much for the past and future. The past is gone, and the future is MINE! So let's address the present: Mind control is a pre-requisite. Spend this time of preparation for India in spiritual preparation by filling the hours with complete focus on the name and form of God. You will find this exercise invaluable to your health and state of mind. Your mind is darting everywhere, wanting to hang on to the past, in fear of the future, and indecisive with the present parting with your home. I will tell you what to do.

"Bring only a minimum of supplies with you. I will take care of your needs. Preparation of your spiritual state is far more important than the physical state.

"Leave your manuscript behind. It has served its purpose. Come straight to me without any preconceived ideas or expectations.

"Your home will be sold in one week, sooner than you thought.

"I want you to come straight over to me, after you close your house... first available flight. (we had planned a months vacation traveling in the U.S.)

"You will stay for a year, play time is over, spiritual time has begun.

"Do not bring a computer.

"This trip will be devoted to spiritual exercises and diet. It will help you to regain health and energy.

"Rent your condo for one year. I will send a suitable couple.

"When Robert retires in May, be prepared to come straight to me.

"Do you hear how clear my voice is within you?"

"Yes, Swami," I replied.

"Follow it. Forget your wants, only want me. I will give you continuous instructions. Don't panic when your desires don't materialize. I'm the Doer - not you. You must first be a good follower before you become a leader. Follow my example always. Don't think even once about failing to live my prescribed path. It will be as I say. I am you, and who are you? You are God. There is no difference. Ask me everything and listen for My reply. Follow the leader. Divine Guidance is your wave length!"

All of Swami's instructions proved to be accurate. We did sell our house in a week and rented our condo. In His instructions He mentioned three times, "come straight over". It was deliberately stated in this manner, as if to emphasize the importance of this instruction.

Twice, before we left for India, I was asked to stay here until after the Sai Mid-West Regional Conference, the end of May. I was asked to Chair the Conference and do a workshop on parenting. I was so grateful that I did not weaken, because the person asking me to stay did in fact present a sound case for me to stay and **selflessly** serve Swami here. But I must obey Swami's instructions, I told her.

Sai tells us, *"When you regard yourselves as devotees of Swami, you have to bring glory to Swami's name. If you behave in a wrong way, you are betraying Swami."* Sanathana Sarathi February '93, p. 36

I was immensely grateful that Swami mentioned it thrice, and allowed me to obey His instructions. My rational mind understood the need here and never knew anything about the advantage of going to India early for Summer School. Thanks to Swami, my "ego" was not sucked in. I had learned from Baba that He is the doer and can work through someone else as well as me. I would have been so disappointed, if I had weakened.

Because of our overwhelming list of chores to be done before we left for one year, neither of us thought about where Swami would be or what He would be doing. To our great surprise, we arrived a few days before Summer School in Brindavan! Swami initiated Summer School this year after ten years absence. Oh, I was so glad we had followed His instructions. We simply had had no way of knowing, but He knew.

This was an extremely powerful learning experience. He taught us to obey His Will even though other circumstances may seem to appear as the right thing to do. His reward, so to speak was our being able to attend Summer School. This certainly induced a strong desire that conditioned our future behavior to respond positively to His inner instructions and obey!

The last day in our house was pulling at all of our hearts. We had lived there for twenty years and now it was time to say good-bye. Robert and I had found Sai Baba in this house and experienced our toughest challenges and greatest spiritual growth there.

Craig was 12 years old when we moved there from Australia, so most of his memories of growing to manhood took place there. And Joan was only 5 years old and all of her childhood memories, her entire remembered life took place there. Each of us were saying our good-byes in our own way.

Sai says, *"The fully blossomed flower fades and falls apart within hours. Even while a person is proud of his physical strength, mental freshness and intellectual sharpness, old age creeps in, with its debilitating effects. And, wealth? And power over men and things: They are like lightning flashes, illumining only a fraction of a moment. They are here today; they are gone tomorrow! These transient natures and possessions, interestingly, produce lasting impressions! Man's enemies are not outside him; the sins he commits are greatest foes. They prompt him to act contrary to all codes."* Thought For The Day, December 28, 1991.

The house and all the possessions that were being carried through the door haunted our minds and sometimes we would stop and reminisce. It was especially hard on Joan, the baby of the family. Craig loved to tease her and gave us all a good laugh.

As I said before, the children took most of our household goods. Since Joan was newly married she could use more furniture than the other children. After everything got unloaded at Joan's house Craig said, "Joan, I don't know why you're upset leaving mom's house, you've got her entire house here!"

In that short statement Craig allowed us to experience the essence of family life. His words spoke of the joy and sadness of living in a family and the cheering up through humor that goes on day after day. It summed up what family truly means to us: concern for each other.

Since I am writing about Swami, including my personal experiences, it is emotionally harder than writing about something other than myself.

As I write and rewrite these different life experiences, I am also going through an internal cleansing because I am forced to relive and look at all issues. And I can tell where my greatest attachments exist because of my emotional response. I know **where** I must do more **Cutting The Ties That Bind**, by Phyllis Krystal.

119

Swami says, *"Everyone must learn the secret of happiness which consists of refusing to shed tears for anything less than God. You have won this human body, this human life, as the reward for many lives spent in acquiring merit. You have won this chance, this unique good fortune of being able to see a holy being, to have the darshan of Sai. Plunging deep into the waters of this tumultuous ocean of time, you have heroically emerged from its depths with the rare pearl in your hands of Sai's grace. Do not allow it to slip from your grasp and fall into the depth again. Hold on firmly to it. Pray that you may have it forever and be filled with the joy that it confers. That is the way you can render this life fruitful..."* Sathya Sai Speaks, 9

This quote always helps me when I begin to get too attached to my worldly life, especially to my family. The children were my life's work and I have been on the job for 33 years, working for the same company. Retirement from the known, change, takes extra effort. I was retiring from the home and Robert from his job. Our life will never be the same. It is not easy letting go. Baba says, *"Past is past, future not known, stay in the Omnipresent."*

I thought, 'Omnipresent, that's new to my ears. What does He mean?' 'Oh... ,' I thought, 'Omnipresent is staying with God in the Present.' How magnificently stated!

I know how hard it was for my children, relations and friends to understand what we were doing. Only a spiritual seeker would realize that this life is temporary and we were leaving in order to attain the **real** object of life, a permanent place in God's heart.

In His Discourse on April 6, 1993, Swami said, *"Attachment is not spiritual. You should have no attachment to children, only to God. Some people are attached to their children even at death. This is very wrong. The only attachment you should have is to God.*

At times our family felt abandoned. Our leaving forced all of us to find our own inner strength because we could not rely on each other. It made us all search and reach out more to God. It had **nothing** to do concerning our genuine love for our family and friends. And **everything** to do with expanding our capacity to LOVE.

Sai Baba said in Kodai, *"Narrow mind is contraction of life. Expanded mind is expansion of life. Empty your vessel, empty your brain of desire and stuff it with the Divine!"* Kodaikanal April 4, 1994

If my vessel, my mind, is continually focused on worldly desires then there is very little space for God to fill it with love energy. This view is the contracted selfish view.

On the other hand, if my vessel, while emptying itself of worldly desires replaces them with God consciousness... I will attain expanded consciousness.

Swami says, *"What can the possession of canvas and paint do, if an artist with vision is not moved to paint? What can the chisel and a lump of marble do with no image formed in the heart of a devoted sculptor? That vision and image are the sparks of the Divine. You are all 'the Divine' packed in human skin and bone, the Atma encased in the evanescent flesh. Know this and you become fearless, happy without limit. Get rid of ego-enclosure in which you now feel you are shut in, then, you are liberated from the non-existent prison which now enfolds you as hard as an existent one! This is the higher wisdom, the knowledge of the Spirit."* Thought For The Day, January 8, 1992

DESIRE

RESISTANCE TO DESIRE; CREATES ENERGY THAT ACCUMULATES UNTIL THERE IS ENOUGH IN RESERVE TO LIFT YOU ABOVE THE DESIRE

DISCOURSE GIVEN BY INNER VOICE.

Everytime you pass a ice cream store and the desire for ice cream is denied, you save money and time which ultimately is reduced to energy. The stronger the desire, the deeper your Samara (worldly life), the longer it takes, the more times you must resist because the energy that is used to lift you above the desire, must equal the weight of the desire.

The Divine Intelligence within you must exert its Will Power to transcend the physical world of senses. It is called WILL POWER because the force that is needed for transcendence is Energy Power coming from the Will. Your desires use x amount of energy to fulfill. The equation is:

Desire (-) action = Energy Saved

Desire (+) action = Energy Depletion

Therefore the less you act on your desires; the sooner you raise your consciousness and evolve from one spiritual level to another.

Imagine a space ship being launched. It uses so much fuel and power at the ground level to create a lift-off. But as soon as it leaves the physical atmosphere, there is no longer a resisting force like gravity. Once the space capsule is in orbit it requires very little energy to maintain it.

The same process is true for raising your consciousness. The greatest effort is at the ground level, the physical level, because you are being tempted by your senses. Maya is like the gravity of the senses. It also, takes much greater power to lift you above the Maya of the material world. Your emotions respond to all outside and inside stimulis which enters the consciousness via the outer and inner senses. Your senses create a feeling because senses feel in order to determine what is happening in the environment. What is felt has an emotional response that motivates your action. Known to you as movement, action, karma, or E - MOTION.

Your emotions are responsible for motivating or persuading you to act on your desires or resist them by allowing the Will Power to take control.

E-MOTION. E stands for Earth. Remove the E and you will receive the motion to lift your consciousness far above the Earth plane. The same is true with E-GO. Remove the E, earth identity, and you GO!

This is the reason why you are told to witness but not respond. You must witness the action on the earth plane but deny any E-motional or E-go response. If the energy does not go outward it remains inward to advance your consciousness level. Your vision is tuned to inward movement not outward.

Detachment is the tool that you use when observing the physical world without responding. You simply cut off the energy supply to respond to the outside. This energy is redirected to inner movement that brings you closer and closer to your real identity, the God within. The closer you become to this Divine Source the greater love you experience which creates within your inner senses, joy, happiness and bliss. This freedom from physical desires or attachments is called detachment which leads to liberation which is freedom from the wheel of life, death, and rebirth.

Inner Voice January 1987

One of the first thoughts that can enter our mind when we hear of Sai Baba, the man of miracles, is the question of anti-Christ. Our family members and friends become fearful of any contact with Sai Baba because they tend to associate Him with what they have heard through the media, on cults, anti-Christ and Satanic organizations. It scares them, and the remedy for fear is knowledge. The obstacle is overcoming fear to read about Him and His words of Divine Love.

As soon as we mention that Sai Baba can perform miracles and has power beyond normal human capacity, like raising people from the dead, healing the crippled, restoring sight to the blind, healing incurable cancer, we tend to believe these accomplishments have only two

125

sources, God or Satan. When we speak of God on earth not in the form of Jesus, it is almost blasphemy for those who have their religious roots in Christianity. It is unthinkable that Jesus would not return as a "Christian".... the only conclusion is that since He cannot be Jesus... He must be the anti-Christ. But how can a being who exhibits Divine qualities the same as Jesus, be an anti-Christ?

We need to have a means of discriminating between good and evil, Divine and Satanic forces that are present in our society. Sai Baba in a discourse described the nature of a Divine personality vs. a Demonic personality.

He said, *Arjuna asked, "Lord! You said that it is the inherent quality of nature that distinguishes these two (God directed nature and demonic nature). Which qualities make a demonic nature and which a God directed nature?"*

"Krishna replied, "Arjuna, I am ever willing to clarify. I only need listeners who are steady and intent. These 25 holy qualities are the traits of the divine endowment. Hear this with unwavering attention:

- *Fearlessness*
- *Purity of emotions*
- *Awareness of the unity of all creation*
- *Charity*
- *Control of the senses*
- *Sacrifice*
- *Study*
- *Asceticism*
- *Straight forwardness*

126

- *Nonviolence*
- *Integrity*
- *Equanimity, absence of anger or resentment*
- *Detachment*
- *Inner peace*
- *Refrain from scandal-mongering and talking ill of others*
- *Sympathy*
- *Absence of greed*
- *Sweetness and softness of speech*
- *Fear of unrighteous acts*
- *Absence of fluctuation in the mind*
- *Courage, patience and fortitude during disaster*
- *Steadiness*
- *Cleanliness*
- *Harmlessness*
- *Humility*

"Krishna continues.... Pride, pomp, vanity, anger, harshness and absence of discrimination are the components of the demonic endowment of mankind. People having these qualities are infused with the demonic character. Though to all outward appearances they may be humans, they do not deserve that name. Those who have the aforesaid qualities are known as human beings with divine parts. Those who have the demonic attributes are known as demonic humans.

"Some people esteem themselves as part Divine, but do they have all the attributes that should characterize them? Do they at least have sympathy, morality, service to others,

and equanimity? If they have these, at least in small measure, they can be regarded as Divine. Instead, if the full battery of demonic equipment is evident in them how can their declaration be taken at its face value? It is sheer vanity to pretend so or to claim such. Vanity and pomp can never be classified as Divine; they are unquestionably demonic.

"Each one can easily analyze and decide to which class he belongs. The classification is not decided by physical appearance, possessions, status or authority.

"For example, consider Ravana. He had a human form; he was an emperor, and he was greater than Kubera, the Lord of Wealth. But can he be considered part Divine for those reasons? No! He is declared a demon on the basis of the qualities he had.

"Three qualities form the fundamental basis of all demonic natures. They are desire, anger, and greed. They destroy the self and foster the demon in mankind. They have to be overwhelmed and overcome by the divine qualities of detachment, equanimity and renunciation. They are the warriors to rely on in this fight. Foster these warriors, and they will, in a trice, wipe out the forces of demonic influence. Any trace of the foes -desire, anger, and greed left unsuppressed anywhere is a potential danger, so they must be reduced to ashes. That leads to real success in the struggle for the goal." Sathya Sai Newsletter Winter 1992-93, p. 23-24

Elaine and David Gries, devotees from Ithaca, New York, give information from two books on cults: "Mindbending: Brainwashing, Cults, and Deprogramming in the 80's" by Lowell Streiker, Doubleday, New York 1984 and "Encyclopedic Handbook of Cults in America" by J. Melton, Garland Publishing, New York, 1986. These are some of the important points they make.

WHY THE SAI ORGANIZATION IS NOT A CULT.

Streiker indicates that a real cult will lack the following characteristics:

- Genuine concern for member's welfare.

- Appreciation of constructive criticism from nonbelievers

- Active encouragement of dialogue between members and the outside world

Beyond that, there are nine major characteristics of cults, as listed below. With each characteristic, we show through direct quotes from Sathya Sai Baba that the Sai Organization does not have these characteristics. In the references for quotes from Baba, SSS stands for the series of books "Sathya Sai Speaks".

1. Primary cult activities are fund raising and recruiting new members.

"I do not like your going about collecting funds or raising donations." SSS VI, 67, p. 325

"Fund collection is as much opposed to this movement as fire is to water." SSS VI, 5, p. 34

"Enough for us if there remain one or two members where practice and preaching are correct and sincere. Quality is accepted; quantity is of no consequence." SSS VII, 13, p. 81

"I do not need any publicity." SSS IV, 23, p. 140

"Do not imagine that your task is to propagate Baba and speak of Baba and His message." SSS IX 35, p. 191

2. Cult members are encouraged to cut off communications with family and friends. They are isolated from the outside world and any reality testing it could provide.

"Your primary task is to discharge your duty. This does not mean renouncing worldly life or your obligations to your family." Sanathana Sarathi, February, 1992, p. 37

"Use the opportunities confronting you as a householder to develop detachment and self-sacrifice." SSS IV, 33 p. 191

"Don't keep yourself separate by working on your own salvation through meditation; move among your sisters and brothers looking for opportunities to help." SSS VII, 39 p. 194

3. Cult members hand over possessions and earnings and become totally dependent on the group.

"Whoever may ask, even if they say that I have authorized them, do not give them a penny." SSS VII, 57 p. 307

"Do not lean on others; live on your own earnings, your own resources." SSS VIII, 44, p. 231

"Where money is asked and offered, I have no place." SSS IV, 69, p. 392

4. The cult enforces demands by peer pressure, embarrassment, and sometimes even violence.

"Humility and tolerance must characterize the behavior of Sai devotees." SSS X, 10, p. 44

"Start the day with love; spend the day with love; end the day with love; that is the way to God." SSS VIII, 14, p. 88

"Non-violence includes not causing hurt even by a word, look or gesture." SSS X, 59, p. 307

5. The cult is the only possessor of truth - others are unsaved and hostile to truth.

*"Do not develop fanaticism or sectarianism."*SSS VI, 7, p.37

"All religions call upon the one, omnipresent God." SSS X, 44, p. 230

"Diversity of religion and faith is conducive to the welfare of mankind." SSS VIII, 25, p. 149

"Finding fault with another's faith casts a slur on yours. " SSS V, 67, p. 333

"You have to teach the equal validity of all faiths. " SSS X, 5, p. 283

6. The cult feels above the law; the ends justify the means of lying, stealing, defrauding.

"Dharma (right action) is essentially social morality." SSS IX, 2, p. 13

"Dharma includes morality, truth, virtue, love, and a host of other qualities that uphold communities of man and the individual." SSS VI, 38, p. 165

"Care of the country is as important as care of the body. SSS VII, 20, p. 98

7. The cult may be apocalyptic; members will be the only survivors of a world catastrophe.

"Do not be upset at calamities; take them as acts of

grace. " SSS V, 32, p. 165

"No disaster is imminent for the world. Over the vast globe, there may be some mishaps here and there, from time to time." Sanathana Sarathi, March 1991

8. The cult is based on the teachings of an authoritarian, corrupt leader who is the sole source of what the group believes and of rules for daily behavior.

"The scriptures lay down the lines along which man has to direct his thoughts and activities. Sincere adherence to those laws and limitations alone can guarantee wisdom." SSS IX, p. 151

"I have not come to set foot a new cult." SSS VIII, 46, p. 235

"Seek out chances to study and substantiate the basic similarities in all religions." SSS VIII, 14, p. 9

"The Vedas are the foundation of Indian culture." Sanathana Sarathi, Dec. 1982, p. 260

"Truth, right action, peace and love are the four pillars of eternal wisdom." SSS III, 25, p. 122

9. The cult exists for its own material survival and makes false promises to help society.

"The Sai Organization is exclusively for spiritual development." SSS VII, 34, p. 164

"Service to man is the best form of worship." SSS IX, 46, p. 235

"Organizations, bearing my name must render service to the helpless, sick, distressed, illiterate and needy." SSS VI, 36, p. 158

Discourse on Cults taken from Sathya Sai Newsletter, Fall 1992, p. 8, 9, 10

YEAR WITH BABA

When we arrived in Bangalore, we heard that Sai was at the Brindavan campus and after an absence of ten long years initiated Summer School again. "The last summer course was held in 1979 for students from all over India. This years course was confined entirely to Sai Institute students. Over 1100 students attended. The guest speakers were a galaxy of leading personalities from different walks of life," stated the Sanathana Sarathi in June 1990. Baba delivered a discourse every evening for the two week course. The topic for this Summer Course was "Indian Culture and Spirituality".

We went to darshan. There is always a 'rush' when I see Swami, after an absence from His Glorious Form. The tears of joy, which Sai calls *"Joy Drops"*, caught in my throat as I mentally thanked Him for all the Blessings He had bestowed on us since our last visit. And when I thought of the opportunity He had given us to stay with

135

Him for a year, the tears slid down my cheeks as I dwelled upon the Majesty of His little brown form. Oh how, my heart cried out as He came near, "Mother, I'm so happy to be home again with you!" His Being floods the entire atmosphere with a sweetness that washes all negativity from my thoughts, and cuddles me in a warm blanket of Divine Love. My heart rejoiced and all I could feel was great gratitude, a spiritual thanksgiving.

Baba says, *"We must love God but even to love Him is a gift from God. We must return the Love to God that He gives us."*

Kodai April, '92.

Afterwards we talked with a few old friends, inquiring about the availability of rooms in Brindavan. We were told that during Summer School all accommodation was for the students and guests. Every place in the village was crowded with devotees, but we both knew that Swami wanted us to stay there rather than in a hotel in Bangalore.

The following darshan Susan Caffery, one of my friends, told me that there was a room being vacated just across the street, near the gate. But we must hurry before someone else took it. We promptly went and booked the room. It was perfect, and they even served three meals a day. We moved in between darshans.

During darshan, Swami called us for an interview. Sometimes you are overwhelmed with the Grace of the Lord. It had been five long years for me since I visited the interview room.

Immediately Swami made vibhuthi for all the ladies. Then He spoke to a young Indian man.

"You're not wearing your ring all the time... I know. You can't wear it while you work. Would you like a chain?"

The man handed Him his green diamond ring. Swami held it between His fingers and blew three times, the ring disappeared and a gold chain appeared. He materialized a beautiful gold chain and motioned for the man to come near and Swami placed it around His neck.

After materializing the chain Swami fumbled with the catch for almost a minute. What a paradox! He materializes the ring in an instant and fumbled with the catch. But how nice it was for the man to get so much close attention from Baba.

A man from Holland knelt up and took off his ring, which was not a ring made by Baba.

Swami took it and asked? *"What's this?"*

The Dutch man asked, "Swami, will you take my ring?"

Swami again held it between His two fingers, blew three times and a magnificent diamond ring appeared.

We heard a day after the interview that the man's ring was the last article he possessed of his wife. They had had a bitter marriage. He asked Swami in his heart, to take the ring if the karma between them was over.

It is impossible to perceive the truth with our senses and make a judgment on these perceptions especially in the 'intensely charged' climate of being with Baba because we are not aware of the motivation or circumstances that created this situation. There is much more than what meets the eye when we look at others actions.

He says, *"Nobody can stand before Swami. Swami knows all. This secret is not known to many. Because our level of understanding is low; we say His level is low. He speaks to us on our level so we can understand but this does not mean that He is not a high level."* Kodai April, 1992

Sai Baba took the man's ring held it up and asked, *"What is this?"*

Different answers came forth, a ring, green stone ring, etc.

"No," said Sai pointing to the ring. *"This is God. God is everywhere. The whole world is in the palm of my hand. The senses and elements like the wind and earth, taste and sight, are all God. Man must control the senses and so be human otherwise he is an animal."*

He looked at me and said, *"Sometimes you control the senses and sometimes you do not."*

His face looked like Shiva, strong and powerful and He spoke to me eye to eye, *"You are MASTER. YOU ARE MASTER."*

Baba was showing me the strength that is within me that I wasn't not using it. I could see the power in His eyes, face and voice. I shall not forget.

He asked the group, *"How do you become God?"*

Again a few replied, "surrender, love".

Swami answered the question, *"By Serving All, you become God. God is Love; Serve others."*

I asked Baba, "What should I do with the book?" Boy did the Lord have fun teasing me!

He asked me, *"Where is the book?"* While He was looking all around for the book.

He continued, *"Do you have it with you? Where is it?"* He was still looking.

'What a joke!' I thought. I brought the book on the last two trips and Swami ignored me. This time He told me inside to leave the book at home. I stumbled for an answer.

"It's in the U.S., but my husband has brought computer discs of the book."

My thoughts turned to the humor of his little play. When I've got it He doesn't want it; when I leave it at home, He wants it. I just loved the game.

He didn't quit, *"What is the name of your book?"*

"I have no name, Baba, I want you to name it."

He threw His hands up saying, *"You have no book, no name..."*

He acted like, "What are you talking about, lady." Everyone was laughing.

By the third time Swami asked, *"What is the name?"*

I felt embarrassed and said, "My mind is blank...... "

He said, *"No, BLOCKED, not blank."*

Again the laughter.

Now Robert came to my aid. He said, "Swami, she won't do anything with the book unless you give her permission!"

Swami said, *"I know."*

He continued the conversation, *"Where is your husband?"* There's that question again, I thought. This time I'd try a different answer instead of pointing to Robert, I'll point to Him.

I said, "You are my husband." He made an awful face, using His hands in a motion of pushing me away.... *"NOT ME,"* He replied.

Everyone is bent over with laughter, except me, I was puzzled.

Baba looked at me very coyly, and said, *"Husband or has been husband."*

Swami's act was hilarious and He did get His point across to me. Sai was letting me know that I still have too much attachment to Robert and as long as this exists He cannot take me.

Swami said in Kodai, *"There is no sofa in the heart, no musical chairs, only ONE CHAIR."*

Then Baba asked me, *"What kind of book is it? Is it social, economical, spiritual..... "*

I hastened to say, "Spiritual Baba."

"What is the book about?" He continued.

"It is about my experiences with You, Baba and how

you have changed my life and helped me to become a more loving person. Also how you have helped my children and my parents." It seemed that He was content with the answer.

"How many pages," He asked.

"Over 200," I replied. Then He gestured for us to come into the private interview room.

As we entered He slapped Robert on the back, in friendship..... as if to say, "How are you my friend?"

We knelt at His Divine Lotus Feet, looking into His eyes. Swami said, *"How long are you staying?"*

Robert answered, "How long do you want us to stay, Swami?"

Sai asked, *"What about your visas?"*

Robert replied, "Thank you, Swami, for our 1 year's visa."

Baba then said, *"I know, I know, you stay for one year. Very happy, very happy."*

He turned a little towards me and asked, *"What is the name of your book?"*

"Please Swami, you name it!"

He waited.... then said, *"Name the book, Vision of Sai."*
"What?" inquired Robert.

Swami spoke slowly and strongly, *"VISION OF SAI."*

Robert and I both repeated the name to confirm it, Vision of Sai.

Swami for the third time said, VISION OF SAI and He drew S A I in the air.

"Who will publish it?" He asked.

"Who do you want, Swami?" said Robert, "someone in Bangalore or Madras?"

Baba replied, *"Printing is very expensive in Bangalore and Madras."*

Swami paused and asked, *"How many copies?"*

"How many do you want, Swami?" asked Robert.

Sai said, *"1000, 2000, 3000, 5000, too many, do 2000 copies. Bring the book to me when it is printed."*

I asked Baba, "Can I take padnamaskar."

He said, *"Yes."*

Robert asked, "What about my monkey mind, Swami?"

"Mad monkey," said Baba.

He patted and rubbed Robert's head in a circle. *"I will take care,"* Sai answered.

Then I asked, "Swami, what about detachment?" (I meant from husband, children and desires)

Baba spoke slowly and with compassion, *"DETACHMENT IS NOT EASY, IT IS NOT EASY."*

He continued very sweetly..... *"One must detach not physically but mentally. Detachment is MENTAL."*

The private interview concluded.

Our wildest expectations could never have prepared

us for this Blessing. Robert took the book discs to Bangalore and had the pages xeroxed. There was a wooden shelf in our room that I used for my desk. I began re-writing almost immediately. What I needed was an editor. I again turned to Susan and she introduced me to Sybil Primrose, who graciously took on the task.

When I started rewriting Vision of Sai, I noticed how the words and phrases were connecting easily. When Swami told me that my mind was BLOCKED, not blank, He meant blocked with fear. I lacked self-confidence. But I must admit that I was not receiving any words of encouragement from those that I sent the manuscript to. I was very happy that Our Lord Sai approved.

Since the interview my self-confidence grew and the fear dwindled through my Master's saving grace.

Summer showers began on May 20th, and the auditorium was jammed 'Indian style.' The guest lecturers spoke to the students during the day and no-one could attend these sessions unless they had a pass from Baba. But everyone could attend the discourse given by Sai Baba at 4 p.m. and every evening we had 'Summer Showers' hence the reason for the summer school name.

Before Swami spoke, He usually invited several students or guests to speak. The boys gave grand examples of Sai Baba's Omnipresence, Omnipotence, and Omniscience. They shared what Swami meant to them in their lives. Swami was everything to them, mother, father, brother, friend and teacher who loved, protected, provided and even performed the miracle of restoring and/or saving a few of the students lives.

One boy was burned by chemicals in the eyes and blinded at the school laboratory while doing an experiment. Swami restored His sight. Another fell from a great height and Sai saved the boy from getting any broken bones.

One afternoon a student shared the following story. It was his first year with Swami and he was in the ninth standard.

He said, "Class was dismissed for the summer, but many of us did not want to leave Swami and decided to stay at Prasanthi. Therefore I made no arrangements to go home.

"After a few days, Swami told me to go home to my parents. I usually tell my parents when I am coming home and they send me a ticket. This time I had no ticket or reservations, and I was afraid of traveling alone.

"I prayed to Mother Sai, "You are my mother and father, my parents from birth always arrange for my ticket. Since they do not know, I'm coming home, You, Swami, must arrange for my ticket."

"When I arrived at the train station there was a large sign saying, 'No more tickets available.' I waited in the long line, worrying, because if I asked for a ticket, the man at the window might get angry with me because the sign in the window said no ticket's available

"When my turn came, I asked the man for a ticket. The man replied, "There is a reservation in your name, and the ticket is paid." This is how much Mother and Father

Sai Loves us. He loves us so very much."

There were hours and hours of Wisdom being taught to the students and guests. There were three statements that particularly touched my heart that I wish to share with you.

Sai said, *"The Avatar only tells man what to do* **indirectly.** *The avatar never tells man what to do* **directly.** *The reason for this is Sai wants you to be your own God, to establish a relationship with the God in you."*

This helped me to understand why Swami seldom gives us direct instructions when we ask Him. Instead we receive the answer via another person, place, or thing. Sometimes we get the answer through the process of elimination or our experiences. He was not avoiding me, only teaching me through my own experience.

The second statement emotionally blew us open! Swami stopped talking then spoke in English with deep sorrow.

> **"God never forgets man**
> **But Man forgets God."**

His tone pleaded with us in an almost pathetic sadness telling us how it feels to be a rejected God. He was reminding us that our ignorance and desires come before Him. It was a spiritual experience that permanently changed my motivation to place Him first in my life, instead of when it is convenient.

Swami told us, *"Some people wonder why He doesn't talk with them? If they do not follow my words, I do not waste my time with them. If they go one way, I go the other way. They are not doing as Swami says."* Summer Showers '90

Swami told me in His instructions before leaving the U.S. to bring no computer. After Sai told me to publish the book, we decided to get a computer and asked Sai with a 'yes' note in the darshan line. We went into Bangalore and priced them. They were more expensive than in the U.S. After doing our market research for the best buy, we decided to purchase one.

After darshan we were going into Bangalore. One of the professors had just come from Prasanthi, and called out to Robert. The professor told Robert where to purchase the computer, and that one of Swami's graduate students was selling them. We did buy one from him and saved money. Just at the right moment, the professor showed up with a name and the information to help us.

The day after summer school, we got a telegram from Pat and Craig saying, "Patricia had a mis-carriage. Would we please ask Swami for His Blessings?

Our hearts sank because we knew they had been trying for sometime to have a child, without success. Then two weeks before we left America she found out that she was pregnant. They were so joyful when they told us and so were we.

The next darshan Robert got a front row and held the telegram up and asked, "Swami, please read?" As they both held the telegram Robert asked Baba, "Will you please Bless my son with another child?" Swami said in a slow methodical voice, *"Yes, I Will Bless."* In August we

146

received a letter from them telling us that Patricia was two months pregnant. We cheered and laughed with the news of this wonderful event.

Swami returned to Prasanthi shortly after Summer School, and we committed ourselves to the jobs at hand. Robert installed the computer while Sybil and I edited day by day for a month.

Sybil was an ex-teacher from Australia. She was excellent and never suggested "radical surgery" on my manuscript. She understood my writing style and my desire to get the text simple to read and understand. She had faith that Swami would guide us. Since she was leaving on July 18, we had a deadline to meet. She was returning to India in October and could help me with any final adjustments.

We were kept very busy with the daily schedule of the ashram, my writing, and Robert had multiple jobs to do on our apartment. We wanted a work station for the computer and a kitchen with counters and cabinets, the bathroom needed repairs and the rooms needed to be repainted. We felt that since Lord Sai granted us permission to be allottees for this apartment, it was our responsibility to maintain it. After all the property is our Lord's and the repairs are our gift to Him for His gift to us. Because of the climate and dirt, the buildings deteriorate rapidly.

I have had sinus and mucus problems for most of my adult life. While in India Swami brought this to a head. It became so severe that some nights I would wake up and not be able to breathe because the mucus was so thick.

147

Just at the correct time, meaning (I was ready and willing) to follow a strict diet, Sundaram, a friend, told me about the mucus free diet she was on. She promptly brought the diet to us. We dropped all dairy foods and starches from our diet. We had great fruits and vegetables available, and I learned how to cook Indian style minus the chilies.

We were both getting an inner cleaning job from Swami. I should say a thorough cleaning job because He worked on us physically, mentally, and emotionally. There were considerable changes taking place simultaneously which produced the right chemistry for an intense learning experience. Believe me the Lord doesn't waste any time getting to the root of our problems.

As the amount of our work load increased and the demand on us for "change" in our home and lifestyle accumulated we became more stressed out. Besides the normal cultural adjustments, we had work being done in our apartment, small living quarters, diet change, illness, re-writing, editing, publishing and the everyday "Ashram-Darshan Games." The Lord was building a pretty hot fire underneath us. In addition to this scenario we had a new problem to work through called RETIREMENT!

Sometime after the six week honeymoon or Robert's yearly vacation time, we both started picking on each other. There had been a joke told at Robert's work about retirees. Breakfast and dinner with your wife is ok, but it's the lunch that does you in!

We finally took time to analyze what was happening to

148

us. Robert had quit work and we immediately came to Sai Baba so there was no prior period of retirement adjustment. Swami, I'm sure, had it planned that way. Not only were we with each other continuously but our living space was reduced to 400 square feet! There was no shopping mall, television, restaurant, etc., for either of us to escape to or find our own space.

Well, it was obvious that our "egos" were both suffering from wanting to "do it our way." Suddenly every decision we made during the day affected someone else. There was no privacy. Before, we had accomplished a harmonious relationship during the evenings and on week-ends but now we had to be on guard all day long. The guys at work were right, it's that lunch that gets you!

I realized that when we came for a 2, 3 or 4 week visit, it was easy to "put up" with any inconvenient living condition. But we were staying for a whole year! This was cause for alarm... we had to adapt to our new lifestyle and this transformation would take some serious inquiry. Each of us felt that the little freedom of doing things according to our own wants or desires was being snuffed out.... and it was!

Robert all of a sudden found himself in an opposite role. I started writing most of the day and I would ask him to help with some of the chores. All of a sudden coming from a role of some stature with his job at work, he finds himself delegated to chores.... I teased him sometimes, saying, "Now look how fortunate you are to get an opportunity to 'really feel' what the house wife who stays at home experiences!" He didn't think it was as

149

funny as I did !!!

Thank God for all the years of preparation that led up to this trip, which enabled us to laugh at ourselves, communicate, inquire within for the spiritual significance, and above all else having the advantage of being in the Divine Presence.

The ashram lifestyle helped us to focus on Baba as we struggled through our ego differences. If we followed Swami's prescribed schedule while at the ashram it granted us quiet time for self-inquiry and the gross distractions from the outside world were kept to a minimum. This atmosphere helped us to keep centered.

We had an interesting experience while there concerning Shirdi Sai. On our first visit, Swami had the garland that we gave Him put around Shirdi Sai's neck, and we couldn't understand why! Then years later when we had our Book of Brigue reading, we were told that we were married and Shirdi Sai devotees, in our last life.

Before we went to bed one night, we discussed the possibility of being Shirdi's devotees. Robert said, "If I get a chance I would like to ask Swami, if we ever had Shirdi Sai's darshan."

The next morning, I went to darshan and sat on my regular chair. There was a very old Indian woman who had been sitting next to me for several months. She could not speak a word of English so our communication was with Sai Ram and eye contact.

This exact morning after I sat down, she took my hand. Put something in it and quickly closed it again. As I re-

150

opened my hand, I saw a medal of Shirdi Sai. After darshan when her daughter came to get her, I tried to return the medal. But her daughter would not accept it. She said, "Mom had gotten this medal from the Shirdi Shrine and worn it for many years. She wanted you to have it so her memory would live on." She had no jewelry that I could see on her but this medal and I felt as if I was taking her most prized possession. They insisted. I was honored, thanked them both and went home with a beautiful gift.

There was no way this sweet lady knew of our conversation the night before. What a wonderful sign from Swami! The circumstances were too obvious not to believe. The combination of these three experiences made us feel certain that we were with Shirdi Sai.

Another day Swami spoke to my inner voice and said, "I call so many but they do not come, but you have come and left all behind to stay with me. I am very happy to have you near. I want you to gain the maximum benefit; therefore time will become precious. How to begin?

"It is simple. Stay as quiet as possible. Keep silent so the inner voice of the Atma can be heard. Food should be given no attention in thought, word or deed. Only think of God.

"The next request. You have lived as man and wife but you are now two individuals not living as one any longer. I will help you to understand. Once man makes a commitment to find his True identity... the process of conventional living is discontinued. You no longer belong to the world; you belong to me. The role of man and wife

151

changes to the role of devotee, the spiritual seeker, the individual and his/her Guru. Go inward, contemplate on me, I will guide you." "Swami," I said, "Will you give us an interview?" "Yes soon," He replied from within. Six days later during darshan, Swami told Robert to "go."

Almost every day, I would rehearse my questions for Swami if we got an interview. I wanted to word the questions in a clear and precise manner. I wanted absolute certainty even though Swami says, *"Love My Uncertainty!"*

This day we had a guest for lunch, finished late and we had only a few minutes to get ready for darshan. We rushed and after I sat down Swami came out.

As He was giving darshan on the men's side He asked me inside. "Are you prepared for an interview today?" He just loves to do the unexpected! 'Oh,' I thought, 'do I have the title page of the book that I want Swami to sign? Do I have a pen?' I quickly looked into my bag. After I found them, I noticed Robert was walking towards the veranda.

Robert had written a note in darshan asking Swami, "Should we sell our condo in the Ozark?" Robert and I had discussed asking Swami about this, but I didn't know He was asking it today.

Robert told me that Swami walked directly to him and took the note.

Swami asked, *"Where is your wife?"*

Robert replied, "She is sitting with the ladies and she has the manuscript with her Swami." *"Go!"* said Baba.

152

We both sat at His Lotus Feet. Sometime within the last five years of being absent from the interview room I thought, 'It would be nice to have a seat right next to Swami's Feet.' Obviously Swami heard it and now He had again responded...... His Omnipresence, always finds the little insignificant passing trivia in our minds. It is this type of nonsensical thinking that no one except God would know - even you forget - until it happens..... then you remember.

In the interview room there were three Austrians and eight Indians who Swami talked to in their native language. Then Swami moved His hand in the familiar circles and a Gold Ring appeared. Swami stuck it right under my nose to look at and I commented, "It's so beautiful Baba!"

He replied, "*It's not for exhibition.*"

In 1983 during our wedding ceremony when Swami made us rings, I wanted a prettier ring like Robert's. Since that day, Swami has taken advantage of every opportunity to make sure I get a good look at the rings He makes for "someone else."

He made the ring for the Supreme Court Justice's son the ring. The ring had three large diamonds. It was an outstanding ring. Ever since my bout of 'ring jealousy', I was so ashamed that I vowed to stamp it out if its ugly head ever appeared in my heart again. To my knowledge it has not but Swami keeps testing me! I am genuinely happy for those devotees who are Blessed to receive His Grace.

"Swami materialized a picture for someone and said, *"If you burn this picture it turns to ashes. If you put it in your pocket it gets tattered and torn. If you drop it in water it gets faded. But if you have Swami in your Heart it is always perfect forever and ever."*

Then Sai looked at me and asked, *"How's your book?"*

I said, "Sai, I sent the book to..... the Sai Publisher in New York." (I got Swami's permission with a yes note before I sent it)

Baba said, *"Very happy, very happy! The printing in America is much better than in India."*

I handed the title page to Swami. He read out loud, *"Vision of Sai, nice name, by Rita Bruce."*

Then Sai Baba asked another man about his health. As His hand quickly moved, I again held my head underneath it. I first noticed what looked like a rock, my first thought was a lingam, but in a few seconds it was recognizable... a large piece of Rock Candy. Swami broke off a piece, passed it to the sick man and instructed him to break a piece off for the next five days and eat it. Then he will be healed.

Baba then motioned for us to go into the private interview room. Swami always asks us what do we want? So we decided to ask Swami this same question if given an opportunity.

"What do you want, Baba?" I asked.

I was not prepared for the emotional tenderness with which our Lord answered.

154

He said, *"ALL I WANT IS YOUR LOVE."*

I mumbled and fumbled with the response saying, "All I want is to be able to give it to you."

Swami then asked, *"Are you fighting with your wife?"*

"Yes Swami," we answered. (because we both were).

I asked Baba, "What do you mean by has-been husband?"

He answered, *"Husband is now a has been husband. He should now follow his wife's spiritual example."*

Then Robert asked, "Swami, you took my note saying should I sell our condo in the Ozarks?"

"Yes," said Baba, *"Sell the condo."*

Robert continued, "Should we live in the U.S., or Australia?"

Sai said, *"Live in the U.S., all your family lives there."*

"Should we live in St. Louis or by the ocean," asked Robert?

Baba answered, *"Live by the ocean. Ocean is Devotion, Ocean is Devotion to God."*

I asked, "California Baba?"

He answered, *"Yes, live by the ocean in California. A place with a view!"*

Swami then held His arms out showing expansion. He looked at me, sweetly, patted my head and said to Robert: *"She wants to live by the ocean."*

I ask Swami my second question, "Can I reduce my medicine?"

"No not yet," said Baba.

I stated that I wanted to be well. "What about the dizziness, Baba?" I inquired.

He said, *"I will make medicine for you, outside and it will heal you."*

Swami got up and I asked Him to sign the book.

He said, *"Outside,"* while pointing to the outer interview room.

Our Dear Swami then gave everyone else a private interview. When He finished He told us, *"Man breathes 21,600 times in 24 hours."* He then proceeded to teach us the "So Hum' mantra. <u>So</u> is pronounced while inhaling and <u>Hum</u> while exhaling. So Hum means I AM GOD.

Swami motioned for the title page in my notebook to sign and held it in His hands till the interview was concluded.

About one week after our interview, Swami gave me an inner interview while I sat in darshan. Swami had told me, He would give me a beam of light by looking into my eyes that morning at darshan. This would heal my sinus, heavy mucus and cough which leads to my choking and hoarseness.

Several days ago I pleaded with Him to get rid of this problem. I asked, "How can I stay here when I'm allergic to dirt and cement?" (guess where the dirt was piled up from all the construction work.... outside our window!)

I was in a front row seat and when Swami came out He looked into my eyes, and I felt His energy go into my right eye, then to the right side of my brain. 'Why brain,' I thought?

The next day while I waited in darshan for His Presence, I thanked Him for healing me and I asked, 'why the brain, Swami?' He spoke through my inner voice. He said, "I must cure the root cause which is mental and in your brain. Then the brain cells will heal the body of all symptoms."

'Is this how you cured my Dad, Swami?' "Yes, I cured Him in the same manner only I did not correct his bad eating habits nor mental attitude. This is why when you ask to be healed for your depression and dizziness, it is not done immediately. What good will it do if I heal you and then because of bad habits, that still exist, you create the disease again? I want you to change your eating habits and mental attitude."

"I will heal you, you will see.

I am you and you are me....."

The day after the interview, Robert realized that California is very large so he decided to start with southern California and asked Swami with a "yes" note. If Swami did not take the note, he would proceed to the next segment of California.

His note said, 'Swami, should we move to the southern California area? Meaning San Diego to L.A.' Swami took the note.

157

Robert and I did not want to be in the publishing business. We actually wanted to give it to a publisher, preferably a Sai publisher and return the profits to a Sai Baba Trust Fund, but this did not happen. After being refused by all the obvious devotees in the U. S. who do books, we were forced to take the task in our own hands. It was apparent that we were to learn all the phases of writing, editing and publishing a book. One day when I was worrying about publishing the book, Swami spoke within and said, "Do not concern yourself with what will be done or how it will be done but that **My Will be done!**"

On the 5th of January 1991, Sai gave us permission to publish the book in Bangalore. Five days later we left for Bangalore in search of a publisher. We were given two names by the ashram, neither were suitable but while talking with the second printer, a man not with the company suggested that we go to Fotoset in Shrungar Shopping Center. He said that they were the best and most professional in Bangalore. His statement got our attention and we went. After consulting with them, we decided to use their company.

It took only one month for the desktop publishing, pictures, artwork, layout, cover design and negatives to be completed, another miracle from Swami, but it took team work and exceptional coordination, not to mention the hours we all labored.

The book was completed a few days before we were to leave. Robert got first row, in his hand was a copy of the book and a letter for Swami offering the books to Him as a gift. As Swami came towards Robert, Baba asked, *"What do you have?"* Robert stood up and replied, "Vision of Sai, Swami." Sai took the letter and blessed the book. Robert said, "Swami, will you please tell Mr. Suri to accept the books for the book store?" Swami answered, *"Mr. Suri knows his business."* Then Swami made Robert vibhuthi and put it in his hand. The books were delivered to the ashram the day we left, on my birthday.

When we came home we put the condo on the market in May of 1991. We put ads in the Chicago, St. Louis, Kansas City, and Lake Ozark papers and never got one call. We listed it with a Real-estate office and not one person came to see it. Swami had given this condo a invisible shield to prevent it from being seen. We took a trip to California in April 1991 and spent three weeks looking for a home. This trip helped to remove most of our desire. Swami did say, "She wants to live by the ocean." This can easily be interpreted as my desire, not His.

Finally we got tired of trying and went back to India, stayed 6 months, came home and in 1992 we tried to sell it with a different Real-estate firm. The same results, no one came to see it! It's apparent that we are not, as yet, prepared to receive what He wanted us to have. Back to India to be with Baba again.

Sai Baba said, *"When Your own very nature is Bliss, why are you hankering for this world?"*

The third year we succeeded, the condo was sold in October 1993.

159

50TH JUBILEE

Sri Sathya Sai Baba fifty years ago announced that He was being called by His devotees. On October 20, 1940, He declared to His family, *"I am no longer your Sathya, I am Sai." "I am going; I don't belong to you; Maya has gone; My Bhakthas are calling Me; I have My work."* With these words Our Beloved Sai Baba began His Avatharhood. Sanathana Sarathi October 1990 p. 253

Months before the Twentieth of October, Swami lit a lamp of love, called the **Prema Joythi** and placed it into a special glass lantern which symbolized peace, love and harmony. The devotees from Andra Pradesh, Sai Baba's home State, took this "Lamp of Love" in Spiritual Procession to every village, town and city, all over the State. This Prema Jyothi, which was carried in a palanquin with temple honors, graced thousands of homes spreading His Message of Universal Love. From this joythi flame of Love all the Sai Baba Centers in the

161

District of Andra Pradesh lit a similar Joythi Lamp.

From this one jyothi flame of Love all the Sai Baba Centers in the district of Andhra Pradesh would light their own Jyothi Lamps. On October 20th, the Fiftieth Jubilee Celebration of Baba's declaration, people from the different districts brought their lamps of love back to the source, Sai Baba.

Our Beloved Baba has told us, *"You can light many lamps with only one flame and the flame never diminishes. The same is true of Love, when it is passed to another it only expands."*

Baba said, *"There is nothing greater or more magnificent than Light (Jyothi). No other object has the power of light. Light alone has the power to dispel darkness. Light has yet another power. Light (or flame) always moves upwards. Even if you keep a lamp in a pit, the light will only spread upwards. The two important characteristics of light are to dispel darkness and go upwards."* Sanathana Sarathi October 20, 1990 p. 282

The History of Sai Baba has been, will and continue to be recorded, more so than any other Avathar in man's existence. We are living and participating in a unique historical period. Never before has God in Human Form been so widely acclaimed. Prasanthi Nilayam is a "living monument" of Fifty Years of Growth and Expansion, in the Sai Baba era. The stark reality of **yesterday vs. today** has never been so vividly contrasted as it was during the preparation for Swami's 65th Birthday and Jubilee Celebration.

Daily, between June and November, I witnessed buildings rising in weeks instead of months. The number of workers multiplied so rapidly, that it doubled the visiting devotees. Supplies, equipment and manpower were trucked into the ashram. I had never seen anything compared to this preparation in the previous years.

No longer were the female workers putting dirt with their hands in pans that were carried on their heads. Now they used shovels and wheelbarrows, these tools were manned by the male species instead of the female head carriers. The handmade bricks were replaced with cement no longer mixed by hand but in mixers that continuously ran night and day. The wooden scaffolding changed to metal. Large steel forms were being hoisted into place by a four or five story crane. The buildings were now built of cement that was poured into the large forms. Day by day as I looked out of our window the old methods of village construction were being replaced with the modern city techniques by leaps and bounds.

The crews worked 24 hours a day, with huge spotlights turning the night into day. In the middle of the night, I would sit in my room and watch history in the making. Only it wasn't being viewed from a TV/ screen, it was live! I was witnessing a new era being born in the Mission of Sathya Sai. The daily scenes were changing too fast.

There were **eight** large apartment buildings constructed in six months. Usually one was built in six months. In addition to the apartment buildings, an elaborate museum, an airport, and an incredible 70 ft.

Hanuman statue were constructed. Street lights were installed, and streets paved, the existing shrines and the Poornachandra Hall were remodeled and all the shops enlarged. All the existing buildings were freshly painted, land cleared and a magnificent brick and wrought iron fence that would enclose the Super Speciality Hospital Complex was built. Every visible inch of the ashram was like a busy bee hive. I had to remind myself that this was not a city but a remote village in South India.

This was the biggest Birthday Party Celebration, in the world and not one single News Broadcasting Station in the United States knew of this event. The "hottest" news item of this Century and no coverage from ABC, NBC, CBS, CNN, etc., etc. It is delightfully humorous that, we, devotees knew something before Peter Jennings, Larry King, or any other news worthy person!

Swami was on the move and I was jolted into the reality of His 60th Birthday statement about a "Quantum Leap." As I witnessed the rapid building expansion for this Birthday I wondered if this could be an indication of what might happen on the spiritual plane sometime in the future? And would I be spiritually ready? He has told us to double-up our spiritual practice. Could this be the reason that Sai keeps His devotees' lifestyle saturated with problematic events to urgently increase our need to focus on Him through the means of suffering and seeking His help?

I was once told by a devotee who asked Swami in an interview, "How intense should our sadhana be, Swami?" Sai replied, *"If you were sitting in a room and a snake*

164

entered, would you take your eyes from the snake?" "No," was the devotee's reply. *"That intense,"* said Sai. I realized that my eyes are focused on Sai but not with the perpetuity that Sai requests.

In October, my inner Sai told me to begin writing this book I complained to Swami, 'the original Vision of Sai is not published, why should I start the second book?'

The next day, we met our new neighbors Robert and Reidun Priddy. They came to our room for a visit. Mr. Priddy told us that he was a writer who had written several books, one about Swami but had not published any yet! There is nothing that escapes our Lord Sai, He knows all our thoughts and is always letting me know!

I asked Swami inside, how can I get quotes for the new book since I only have a few with me? The answer came as promptly as before. Mr. Priddy told us that he had a 100 page index on all Sai subjects as well as the essences of these subjects, cross indexed with Swami's books. The next morning before darshan, I asked my husband to ask Mr. Priddy if I could borrow the index. After darshan Mr. Priddy came to our room and offered me a smaller version of the index. I asked him, "Did Robert ask you for the index?" He said, "No, I haven't seen him." "Well, I asked Robert one and a half hours ago, to ask you if we could borrow the index." Mr. Priddy replied, "One and a half hours ago, I put it in my bag for you."

That evening he brought me the original 100 page index which was out on loan, and said we could make a copy. Swami was indeed bringing me all the tools that I needed. I was the one resisting. I just wanted to enjoy the moment, the goal... finally reached. I was not mentally prepared to set before myself the goal of writing another book! He was nudging me.

The third Omnipresent occurrence happened with a young girl from Chicago, Monica. For days I had been chewing over the idea of doing a comparison interview called "Then and Now" for the new book with an old devotee in remembrance of this Auspicious occasion, the Fifty Years Jubilee.

Monica knocked at our door and explained that she along with some Chicago devotees were instructed to bring us the "Book and Service Exhibit" from the United States for the World Conference. We were responsible for setting up the exhibit. She said, "The exhibit was in the EHV Building and would we please come to inspect the exhibit and make certain that it was delivered complete, and then they wanted to take some photos."

While talking to Monica, I discovered that she was a reporter. I immediately thought maybe she could help me with an interview. When I asked her she was delighted to help, as long as I did the writing. It was a deal!

The next step was finding someone to interview. I sought out our old friend Mr. Narsimhan, the Editor of Sanathana Sarathi. I asked him, "Do you know a devotee who has been with Swami a long time, because I would like to do an interview for my next book on Swami "Then vs. Now?" He said, "Yes I do, but I must first get his permission. Come back in a day."

When I returned he told me that Judge G. K. Damodar Row would meet with me, he was 89 years old and had first come to Swami in 1960, thirty years ago. 'How perfect,' I thought.

Robert and I went one evening to meet with the Judge and his sweethearted, wife, Padma. There was almost an instant friendship between us which has deepened since our first meeting. Coincidentally, after talking with them we discovered that in 1985 we had been in an interview with them, when Swami made Padma a lingam for her health. Robert recalled all the details, and they confirmed what he said.

Nothing in our life is left by chance, it is a well designed plan and all the parts are connected to the whole. How comforting it is to know that our fragmented, and sometimes confused life really have a supreme purpose and divine planning. The older we become the more exposed we are to the plan and if wisdom accompanies our experiences we can eventually see some of the karmic lessons we are working on in this life.

There has been an immense change since the early days of Sai Baba and because this October 20th, marked the 50 years since the announcement of Sai Baba's Mission it was appropriate for us to reminisce. Judge and Mrs. Damodar Row shared with us the memorable experience of their first journey together to see Sai Baba. Padma Row made her first trip to Sai Baba, several years earlier in 1956.

As told to us by the Judge. "I read a book on Swami called "Sathya Sivam Sundaram" by Kasturi and I knew

167

that this was a Great Soul. So in April 1960, I announced to my family members that I was going to see Sathya Sai Baba and invited them to join me. My wife, brother, children and some cousins, altogether 14 members of my family traveled to Puttaparthi.

"Of course in those days traveling to Puttaparthi was not as convenient as it is today. We traveled by train then a rattling old bus, then a bullock cart was used for the latter part of the journey. This included crossing five miles of a dry lake, and then crossing the Chitravathi River entering Puttaparthi Village near the Shiva Temple. The women traveled in the cart while the men walked behind as they held on to the cart. Since the journey was very difficult only very earnest people would come to see Swami. The curious type of people did not come.

"In those days the ashram was called "Sai Baba's Ashram," the name Prasanthi Nilayam came much later. The Mandir was there, but not so well built and there was no sculptured art work at that time.

"When we arrived, there were about 300 people both men and women waiting to see Swami. During our first darshan, Swami came right next to me and put His left hand on my head, meanwhile he called other people for an interview, but not me. So after bhajans and darshan we had to attend to our belongings.

"There were no hotels or rooms for rent then. We lived under the tree. We cooked over an open fire, bathed in the river and slept under the stars. It was glorious sleeping under the tree especially on a moon lit night. But there were snakes and scorpions there. We never found a snake but we did encounter a scorpion. We would simply put our faith in Swami, each night before we slept we would ask Him to protect us. Then we slept nicely.

"We arose early at 6 a.m., had our bath in the river, drank a cup of hot coffee, then hurried for darshan at 7 a.m. Then Swami would come out and select people for an interview. I had hoped that I would have some luck with Swami and be called. But each day Baba continued to put His hand on my head while calling other people. This went on for seven days. We were not called.

"I told my wife to pack up the vessels because tomorrow we would have to catch the train by 11 o'clock. There was absolutely no hope now for an interview but maybe next time.

"But after Swami finished the morning interview, He surprised us and called *"The Madras Party!"* That was the name He had given us. The first thing Swami did was to greet me by saying, *"You're angry at me."*

"Then the interview was held in the old room, small, three fourths the size of the present interview room and there was no little room in the rear. Swami gave us a beautiful interview. He told us, "*We should love God early in life, and teach our children about God. Husbands and wives should not waste time quarreling.*" He called me *"Bangaru"* and said *"You come back soon."*

"In those days, Swami would give formal darshan but then He would come out and talk to the devotees anytime He felt like it. Sometimes He would come by and ask, *"What have you cooked today?"*

169

"In the evenings, we would sit around the fire and share Baba stories. Those intimate devotees who knew Swami when He was fourteen years old would tell us of His leelas at the wish fulfilling tree. They told us that once Swami stood in the tree and magnified Himself (5000 times greater) until He was touching the sky. Swami was very playful. There was one devotee who would put Swami on his shoulders and run with Him like Hanuman. Another old devotee used to say that Swami gave him darshan as Sai Krishna. Baba performed vast miracles then."

We so enjoyed listening to the Judge's stories, knowing full well that there are but a few "early devotees" still alive to share these priceless precious moments in the life of this Avatar.

Such Glorious Years they enjoyed. Remembering the times of how Swami came and stayed in their home, walking into the kitchen as she prepared the meals in such a friendly manner, just like one of the family. Sai Baba loved to sit on their grassy yard with family and friends all around, answering their questions and showering His joy and bliss on them. Those days are gone forever, it is a past era, and we can only dream of how it must have been.

The 20th of October arrived and Swami's Golden Jubilee was a Glorious Celebration. As I sat in my chair, I thought what did the Lord have planned for us this morning? He was always surprising us with unusual festivities. Swami seemed to delight in entertaining us and His joy spread to us. It was fun to be there with him for this Auspicious Occasion.

Fifty years ago Swami proclaimed His mission by telling his family *"I don't belong to you. I have not come for your sake. I have my own work to attend to..."* As He sat on a boulder, He sang, *"Manasa Bhajare Guru Charanam"* ... *"Meditate, oh mind, on the Feet of the Guru, they can take you across the difficult sea of Samsaara."* Easwaramma, p. 62 & 63.

As Swami came out this morning, a student began singing "Manasa Bhajare" and all the devotees joined him. The song poured forth from all hearts in remembrance of the Love He has given to us during these fifty years. The sound started with one voice and soon the entire atmosphere echoed the sound of many. "Dusthara Bhava Sagara Tharanam." My Heart was so full of joy to be here, experiencing this moment, fifty years later, singing the same tune that marked a historical moment in the Life of this Avathar.

The Mandir grounds were decorated with brilliant colors, it made you feel the merriment of the moment. Swami spoke to a man who ran out of the ladies gate. Then Swami walked on the Veranda, but He kept looking over His shoulder towards the gate. Every time Swami looked so did everyone else! What is He looking for, I thought?

Suddenly the festivities began as we heard the sound of the Marching Band as it came through the ladies gate. We were being entertained by a Grand Parade given by Swami's home State of Andhra Pradesh! Each District had their own contribution to this parade and they individually decorated and entertained Bhagavan with pictures, music, costumes, dances performed by the Bal Vikas children, flowers, streamers and elaborate altars and carriers for their "JYOTHI LAMPS OF LOVE" that they each returned and presented to Swami as He sat in front of the Ganesh Circle. Behind His chair was a towering design of a bright lamp and flame decoration. Hundreds of devotees from Andhra had come to offer their homage to their Divine Guru who had lit the lamp of devotion in their Hearts.

The Jyothi Lamps from each district were lit from the one Lamp that Swami originally sent from the Mandir, months ago. This act was symbolic of how His Love and Mission has expanded since its humble beginning, and its voluminous growth through the millions of devotees who are a "Lamp of Sai's Love" shining in all countries of the world.

After 45 minutes of watching the parade of lights, the last Jyothi Lamp, in a place of honor was sitting on top of a float all decorated in flowers. This was the original Lamp of Prema that Swami sent to Andhra Pradesh, months ago. In conclusion Swami received the Arathi with this flame.

In the evening we were His guest for a discourse that was held in the Mandir Grounds. Swami instead of speaking from inside the Mandir, chose the center of the veranda directly under the balcony. He said, *"The name of Prasanthi Nilayam has spread to all parts of the globe. People from all countries are coming here. Prasanthi Nilayam has become a mini-world. What has been*

172

accomplished here in fifty years could not have been achieved in five hundred years. The Supreme power of attracting so many from all parts of the world can only belong to the Divine. You are going to witness many more things by November 23.

"If you have been able to carry these lamps from house to house, it is not the result of something external. The light has come from your hearts. Hence, more than lighting the lamps outside, develop the jyothis within you and purify your hearts. No government, no bombs, no tanks can save the world. Devotees alone are the protectors of the world."

CHRONOLOGICAL HISTORY OF SOME EVENTS

1945 Paatha Mandir(old temple)

1950 New Mandir - Prasanthi Nilayam

1958 Sanathana Sarathi

1968 First World Conference

1969 Anantapur and Brindavan Campus Open

1972 Annual Summer Courses

1974 Poornachandra Auditorium

1975 Second World Conference

1975 50 Foot Commemoration Pillar of World Faiths

1980 Third World Conference

1981 Education in Human Values

1981 University at Prasanthi & Administrative Building

1983 World Rally of Bal Vikas Children

1984 World Rally of Sai Seva Dal Workers

1984 Trayee Brindavan

1985 Fourth World Conference
1990 Fifth World Conference

65TH BIRTHDAY

The Birthday preparations were in full speed, everywhere it was self-evident that the crowds of devotees would soon be coming to help celebrate the 65th Birthday of Our Lord Sri Sathya Sai Baba. In an Australian interview on November 6th, Swami asked:

"Who is going to be here for Birthday?" He was excited just like a child who was having a Birthday Party. He continued, *"Swami has invited everyone, every devotee.... not just delegates, everyone is invited."* Then He said:

"Hundreds of lakhs will come
It will not be easy
Everyone must adjust
You are all brothers and sisters
Everyone must adjust
Everything will be allright
Don't look for comfort
*But look to the **comforter**"*

175

He continued, *"Some rich people come to see Swami. They want comfortable beds, comfortable sofa, like a hotel. They even want air conditioning. Maybe a cool body but hot head!"*

This Birthday experience would test even Swami's most self-controlled devotees. If you had any expectations, it would be better to park them at the gate before you entered because this would be an experience of sacrifice. How many times our Lord has asked for our Love and this is given through Sacrifice. There were many devotees who knew that this trip would require everything they had learned and spiritually practiced, plus more. It could be a stick to measure our strengths and weaknesses by.

Baba tells us, *"Sandalwood gives more and more fragrance when it is subjected to more and more grinding, so does sugarcane yield juice as it is chewed more and more. Gold gets refined when it is burnt and melted in fire. So also a true devotee will never falter in his love for God even when he faces troubles and obstacles in his life. God tests His devotees only to lift them up to a higher level on the spiritual ladder. A true devotee leads a sacred life which is sanctified when he faces the obstacles and problems with full faith in the Divine. The body is only for leading a sacred life."*

They were predicting half a million or more people in this small village of Puttaparthi. Why did the devotees come even though they knew of the difficulties? The simple fact is, "He asked us·to come." He gives us EVERYTHING, this was an occasion for us to **give** to Him.

He invited every devotee from every land to join in His celebration of three Auspicious events, the 50th year of His Mission, His 65th Birthday, and the 5th World Conference. He promised to feed and house everyone free, as His guest. Those who "Truly Heard His Call" came.

I asked Judge Row to share some of his thoughts with us concerning this momentous event. He said, "The 65th Birthday is a challenge. It is inconceivable to think of the numbers that are predicted to attend, 15 laks. Included in this is a floating population, the village people who will come and go.

"I see this Birthday Celebration as a 'Test of Loyalty to Swami'. There will be many reasons for coming. Some will come out of curiosity, others will come for the food because Swami said, "He will feed everyone free for six days." But Swami wants a meaningful crowd, not a merciless crowd. He wants us to double-up our love and affection for Him."

It was my first time being here for Akhanda Bhajans, 24 hours of singing to Our Lord. It started at 6 p.m. on Saturday and ended at 6 p.m. on Sunday. Swami lit the Akhanda Jyothi in the Prasanthi Mandir and inaugurated the Bhajans. After some time I returned to my room for a few hours sleep but returned at 1 a.m. I sat on the ladies veranda in a chair right in front of the window where the statue of Shirdi Sai was located and I could see Swami's chair.

After hours of singing, soaked in the vibrations of the Bhajans, my being felt as if it was humming with an incomparable peace and tranquillity. Swami lived upstairs, so near. We knew He could hear. I knew and appreciated the fact that this was another priceless gift He had given me. Very often during this year I felt so blessed.

Around 5:30 a.m. Swami gave us darshan through the inside windows on the men's side of the Mandir. He lingered at all the windows blessing us with his Presence.

After His darshan, I decided to go in the Mandir grounds to meditate and when I turned the corner from the veranda, I suddenly saw one second row seat left. I hurried and put my cushion down just in time. I had no idea that people were already coming for morning darshan and there would be no lines. I was lucky that I left the veranda when I did.

Since I sit on the chairs everyday, I didn't have much opportunity for getting close darshan. I wanted a first row seat because I knew the Birthday crowds would make it impossible, and I wanted a close darshan to remember in honor of His Birthday. I asked the devotees in front if they would make a space for me because there was plenty of room but they declined. Then just two seats down from me in the first row, one girl left. Just then Swami came out and I flew into her spot! When she came back, we all made the "darshan adjustment" squeezing closer together so I had a first row.

What a captivating darshan. He walked in slow motion going to the men's side first. It was 6 a.m. and the quiescent sun was just rising. The earth felt sweet, fresh and clean. He took no letters nor did He give

178

padnamaskar. Instead He looked at us intensely, as if He longed to be with us. His aura sweetly purified us with His undefiled, white, bright light! I felt immaculately clean.

The girl whose spot I shared had to leave after darshan therefore, I decided to stay, maybe He would do this again. I kept waiting because Swami was "going in and out" but staying on the veranda. I asked my inner Swami, "Should I leave?" "No, wait," He replied, "I will give more darshan." About twenty minutes passed and I was beginning to doubt what I had heard; I inquired again. He said, "wait,..... wait, I'm coming." "Yes, mother," I replied.

Surely as faithful as the sun, He returned and this time gave me a sweeping long look, straight into my eyes.

During the late afternoon akhanda darshan Swami sent the boys out carrying packages and more packages. Swami was giving saris for His Birthday to the ladies. The college girls and high school girls, the teachers were next, then came the teachers wives, the staff wives, the doctors' wives, the canteen personnel, let me see did I leave anyone out? Yes, Me !

But how did Swami give these gifts out? With the Love of 10,000 Mothers. Each recipient was handed the sari personally by Swami and had padnamaskar. He even stopped to ask them their choice of color. If they received green silk last year with a beautiful border of blue and gold..... He would go back into His room and bring them a purple silk one. Or if the woman wore only a white sari, back to His room He would go and bring her a special white sari. He gave different cloth and different styles according to their ages and stages of life. He even

179

opened some and held them up for all to see, the fashion and designs. The ladies would laugh..... Swami even knew when someone was missing. He would send a Seva Dal to fetch her. The lady would come and Swami would shake His finger at her, so sweetly, letting her know that it was important to Him to have her there. I could go on but I will conclude the sari story in one sentence. "In all of heaven and all of earth, the most desired and treasured gift for a woman is when she appears dressed and wrapped in His Cloth for His Glory."

Next on His agenda came the 'parade of prasad'. About thirty minutes before the closing of the akhanda bhajan, the energy swelled and the excitement grew, not a face showed any sign of weariness. He selected about twenty boys from the veranda and they ran off.

I amused myself thinking, 'what's next?' The boys came back carrying bright, shiny new silver pots, bigger than buckets looking more like fancy serving dishes with a lip, only very, very large. They were heavy because the boys strained to carry them. They came two by two, I counted about 54 silver serving pots. It wasn't the end. The parade of food continued. Huge cooking vessels which reminded me of the big aluminum, washing tubs, the round fat ones, my mom used. Next the boys carried stacks of paper leaf plates (dried leaves stitched together with little wooded slivers) and several buckets with big new silver serving spoons. Just minutes before the closing Arthi came the finale. The final vessel of food was round and large. It took 10 college students to carry it.

All the devotees, lined up in Indian fashion seated on the ground back to back, each given a paper plate. Now, I discovered the reason for the large number of vessels. We were being served a Meal! No cooking tonight "Sai Savories" was the 'fast food' for our delight.

In celebration for the Fiftieth Golden Jubilee of Sri Sathya Sai Baba's Mission there was to be an Overseas Exhibition of Photos and Sai Literature. All countries were invited to participate. In the United States, the Mid-Western Region was assigned this project. They requested all centers to send photos that they had taken at their center activities. There were three categories: service, devotion, and bal vikas.

It was another one of Sai Co-incidences that my daughter-in-love (Sai says, *not mother-in-law, mother-in-love*) and son were selected to head this project for the Belleville and St. Louis Centers who were responsible for the North American entry. Therefore when the project was completed they sent it to us to assemble.

Patricia is very artistic and designed a collage of pictures that were placed in the shape of the United States on a large foam board, with two adjacent panels that were done in a side profile of Swami's face. (see photo) The center panel was all service pictures, devotion and bal vikas were respectively on each side panel. All the St. Louis area devotees worked to assemble this beautiful display of Sai Activities in our country.

Robert attended a Central Co-ordinators meeting since he wanted to know what to do with the exhibit. He was informed of a meeting of the Exhibition Committee to be held at the EHV Building the following day. We both attended the meeting and since there were no names assigned to this committee from the United States we were drafted.

Several days before this event took place, we were going to disassemble the computer to make room for taking in two more devotees because rooms were at a premium. But I was told by Swami inside that I should not take the computer down as I had planned, but leave it up and use it. Well, I was not sure what this would involve.

Gayle Alden from the U. S. was staying with us during the Birthday and a young couple from Australia, Wendy and Robert Cameron I also invited, because they were being vacated from their room. But now I had to tell them no. I prayed that they would understand my message from Swami.

As I was walking up the steps they were looking for us because they had to move today and go to the sheds. They were so sweet and understanding as I explained there would be no room with the computer up. While we were talking in our room, Robert suddenly remembered that we were keeping a key for a neighbors room who was having work done. The work was almost finished and the owners would not arrive for several days. It would be perfect for them now and it was only two doors from us.

Wendy asked me when she passed in darshan that afternoon if the room was clean and could they move in after darshan? I told her yes, but knew that the room would not be cleaned because Parvati could not do it

182

until after 6 p.m. After darshan, I checked on the room and found that Parvati had just finished cleaning the room. What a wonderful surprise and just in time for the Camerons to move in.

Wendy and I had several of these Sai incidents in the following days. I was very busy working for the exhibition and had no time to cook lunch. Wendy came over for a visit and the inner voice said to ask Wendy if she could help me with lunch for a few days? Finally I got enough courage to ask. She was blown away. She said, "I've been asking Sai what kind of service, I could do?" She cooked our main meal and Gayle did the dishes, shopping and some chores. They both helped to unburden us. We were a happy family working and sharing together.

Two days later Swami told me at darshan not to have Wendy cook today because I had a cold coming and should only eat fruit. I went to Wendy's room to tell her. She said, "Wow! I just told Sai I didn't know how I could cook today because I am working in the canteen." These types of experiences with Sai is what makes His devotees absolutely convinced of His Divine Omnipresence.

To continue with our story about the exhibition committee: At the meeting the following day, the chairman, Leonardo said, "We need signs for the various Regions and Countries." I said, "We have a computer and could make the signs." "You have a computer here?" "Yes," I said. "That's wonderful," he replied. We made the signs.

I needed some special work done on one of the signs and was introduced to Shanti, a very petite, quiet mannered woman sitting on the floor in the EHV building working. She asked, "How did you make the sign?" I told her about the computer. She asked, "Can I use it to do my husband's typing because he is the Chairman for this Fifth World Conference?" I asked, "Who is your husband?" "Jagadeesan," she answered.

I chuckled and told her that my husband had just told me as I entered the EHV building that Jagadeshan had requested the use of the computer and he wanted to meet me so I could meet his wife.

During this first meeting of the exhibition committee and workers we found out that this project had to be completed in five days. The first major obstacle was that the 'building' for this exhibition would be a tent. After seeing the tent material and getting the dimensions, a plan was drawn. The big question was how to hang wall exhibits in a tent.

The next day the tent was assembled but to our surprise there was only a half wall around the tent. There was the normal ceiling of the tent but the walls were draped in a heavy fabric that was only half way to the ceiling, and the rest was open. Our Baba was already giving us challenges.

That night a severe storm, highly unusual for India hit Prasanthi and dumped a lot of rain. So many of the devotees were sleeping in the open, on the roof tops and the ground. Everything they brought got soaked including themselves. When we went to our morning meeting, we noticed that the storm had torn down the tent, it had collapsed.

That day Leonardo checked with Swami to see if we couldn't use the EHV building for our exhibit. Swami gave us permission but we had to conform to constant changes.

Sai says, *"Develop Prema (Love) towards the Lord, the Parama-Prema (Highest Love) of which He is the embodiment. Never give room for doubts and hesitations, for questions, to test the Lord's Prema. My troubles have not ended; why? Why is it that He did not speak to me? How is it I did not get a room for staying here? Why did He not call me? You whine! Do not think that I do not care for you or that I do not know you. I may not talk to you, but, do not be under the impression that I have no prema. As a matter of fact, it is to give you the chance of darshan (to see a holy person) that I move along the veranda from this room to that. Whatever I do, it is for you, not for me. For what is it that can be called mine? Only you."* Sanathana Sarathi May 1993

We were told that Swami may inaugurate this Exhibition Himself and if so, it would be on the morning of the 18th or 19th of November. There was never any definite date. We were also told that if we used the EHV building it was already scheduled for a 300 Indian Delegate Meeting that would take place right in the middle of the two opening dates. The meeting was for the afternoon on the 18th. So we would have to set-up for the 18th morning then remove the floor exhibitions to the side for the delegates meeting and again set up that evening and work through the night if needed.

Because of heavy rain for the next two days, the

overseas registration had to move inside with us, so we had to share floor space with the book and photo exhibition artists and workers who were making posters.

There were 29 exhibits sent but only two completed. Many countries sent pictures but they all needed to be artistically mounted and some explanation of the photos and names of the countries they represented. We used hundreds of poster boards. Artists were drawing borders and doing calligraphy. The first day we had one ruler to be used between 10 groups of workers. The next morning 15 appeared.

Each region and country had a sign for their exhibition. After I had them printed out on the computer, they needed to be colored in the country's colors. On the first day, I had requested colored markers. When I finished the signs, it was late - almost 9 p.m. the following day. I said, "Swami I have 20 workers coming in the morning and I have no markers yet." At that exact moment someone knocked on the door and handed me the markers.

Since the exhibition hall was so crowded, we volunteered our apartment for the committee's 8 a.m. meeting, and I also used it for my workers. We had 20 people from all nations working in every inch of that apartment. Since we could not communicate very well, we sang Bhajans. The atmosphere was filled with His Prema.

The leader, Leonardo, was an excellent role model of leadership. He never interfered with the committee unless there was a needed change. We all reported in each morning at the meeting. The committee worked in complete harmony. All who participated in this exhibition experienced a spirit of commitment, trust, love, friendship and positive attitude even under stressful and sometimes impossible conditions. Sai taught us what can be accomplished in a very short period of time when our egos are surrendered and we work as one for Him.

He said, *"Ego is like an inflated football. When one is inflated with the air of ego, both the good and bad qualities kick the body. The moment ego is gone, the kicking stops and one attends to his legitimate duties with the feeling that he does not do anything but is only an instrument."* Sanathana Sarathi May 1993, p. 126

One thing that astonished this newcomer, never having worked on a project at Prasanthi before, was the gigantic tasks that the devotees promised to accomplish in five days. I couldn't believe the size of the jobs that they consented to do in less than five days. Some examples: They made 90 flags, one for each nation to be hung on the wall surrounding Swami's chair, each name beautifully inscribed by a lady who had cancer.

The Thailand ladies spent 3 days and nights working with 40 lbs. of fresh flowers, some sent from Thailand for decorations. They were responsible for flower decorations in the hall, on the altar platform and around Swami's chair. The designs were befitting the King of the Universe. They had sprigs of orchids, floor designs of the sarva dharma symbols, happy birthday spelled out in flowers, plus many other floral designs, garlands, and wreaths for Swami.

We had 400 pieces of Sai literature and photos from 31 countries to display. We had helpers from every profession and country: artists, craftsmen, carpenters, laborers, architects, florists, etc.. At times we broke into small groups. Although there was a language barrier, we spoke the language of the heart. Our eyes and hands spoke of love as we labored for His Birthday Party. When the work was completed the pictures and numerous books told the story of how His Mission has spread in Fifty Years to every nation in our world.

At one of our morning meetings, Leonardo talked to us about singing for Swami. There were seven men and seven women of the committee who could sing, the only exception was my husband, Robert. So he was assigned the job of handing Swami His Birthday Card from all the nations.

The next morning we decided we would sing "Lord of The Universe" written by Loraine Burrows, a committee member. We would practice in our room every evening at 7 p.m. Someone asked if I had a harmonium to use for practicing. I said, "No" but as our morning meeting progressed there was a knock on the door. I had forgotten that I told a devotee I would store her harmonium in our apartment while she was away.. She was bringing it to me. No-one reading this book could have any doubt by now of His Divinity? Right!

The computer was used everyday and even ran for 24 hours without stopping one day. When it was used at night, we just closed the door to our living area and the devotees could use the small entrance room where we had the computer desk. Many countries were writing reports from the Fifth World Conference and copying the Sai Discourses. The miracle was that not once was our building without electricity while others were. During the 60th Birthday, our room had continual 'black-outs'. But this time He gave us His Miracle of Love. Not once did we lack electricity.

"My Love is My greatest miracle. All should share in this love. Then it becomes one. All of you should strive to develop the Seva Organization from day to day. Let all join the organization. Treat all of them as the children of God. Serve them in that spirit. You will experience Divinity very soon. Swami's Love will be with you always, in you, beside you and around you," declared Bhagavan Baba in His Valedictory discourse to the Fifth World Conference of the Sai Organization on November 24th, in the vast Hill View Stadium.

We did not know until after Bhajans on the morning of the 19th of November that this would be the day that Swami would inaugurate the Overseas Book and Photo Exhibition. Leonardo asked Swami and He said, *"Yes!"* We were so excited.

When Swami came to the Exhibit on this day, we were prepared. The Hall was magnificent. Never did I dream that so much work could be accomplished in such a short time. The transformation was unbelievable.

Swami got out of the car... we started singing, "You are Lord of the Universe." He was greeted by our Chairman, and garlanded with red roses. He walked up and down the road giving darshan to the ladies and men who had gathered there. He was so sweet. He walked ever so slowly to a little girl with a tray of sweets which He blessed and threw to the devotees. He then accepted a rose from a little boy.

As He ascended up the stairs He walked on a red velvet carpet covered with rose petals. As He passed the group singing, He joined in with us and looked at Loraine.

In the foyer entrance were two large maps mounted on frames, standing opposite each other. On one World map Swami could see the locations of the International Sai Centers, 1073, each dotted with a mini-picture of Sai. On India, we had placed the lotus feet of Swami. Swami pointed this out to His guest walking with Him. The opposite map was of Latin America with a huge rainbow coming from India and covering Latin America and all their centers were marked. We had also made a large chart that showed the number of centers in every country overseas.

At the foot of each map were lit candles in glasses, and deep red velvet cloth runners which held flower designs spelling "VERY HAPPY BIRTHDAY".

Five hundred colorful balloons were strung around the entrance of the exhibit, after all this was a Birthday Party. (The night before the helium gas tank did not show up so we had to blow them up by mouth!)

As Swami cut the ribbon and walked into the building, rose petals were released from a gold bag that hung from the ceiling and the petals fell to His feet. He lit the Arthi Lamp, Blessed the coconut water, and received from Robert a large white card with HAPPY BIRTHDAY written

190

on it in gold letters. He carried this card throughout the entire ceremony, never handing it to someone else to hold. **As if to remind us that He is always with us carrying each devotee from each nation in His hands.**

An architect from Spain had been in charge of decorating the building. The ceiling was decorated in a "May Pole" fashion with crepe paper and newly made cloth banners hanging from the ceiling with gold foil letters shimmering the five values; Truth, Right Conduct, Peace, Love and Non-Violence. There were also banners of artistic designs and Swami pictures, and the banners that hung in the windows were co-ordinated with the ceiling ones.

The red velvet carpet with rose petals went across the exhibition hall to His chair, and the altar was decorated with a Flag of every nation, flowers, and candles. Swami accepted from one student a summary book that included every book in the exhibition listed according to country and author.

As Swami looked at the exhibitions He talked to the representatives that were posted at each country's display and He remarked on the pictures.

When He came to the Latin American exhibition, He paused. There was a photo of the President of Guatemala and his wife who were attending a Sai Baba Conference. The President's wife was in the photo drinking from a champagne glass. Swami pointed to the photo and said, *"I told them I would be there, see there I am!"* He pointed to the proof that was in the photo. You could see Sai Baba's full body lying in the bottom of the wife's glass in the photo! What an extraordinary photo which we did not see until He pointed it out. There was Swami's face, hair and body curved to fit in the bottom of the champagne glass.

Leonardo asked, "Swami, may we have Padnamaskar?" Swami replied, *"Certainly!"* The ladies were sitting on one side of the red carpet runner and the men on the other. His Divine Lotus Feet were given in a slightly unusual manner. As He walked down the carpet, His right foot was given to the ladies and the left was given to the men. He would hold His right foot out, then His left foot, lady, man, lady, man, etc. We all wanted to have Birthday Padnamaskar and He granted our wish. As He departed we sang arthi. Swami was pleased with the exhibition. He said, *"Very, very happy!"*

His love and sweetness blissed everyone out and was captured on a photo taken by Allen Woods for each of us to remember. Allen had told us that he was going to take a picture of Swami in His chair, but he had to wait till his flash re-charged. Swami started to get up but noticed Allen and sat back down until he could take a picture.

During these five days of preparation, the goals sometimes seemed impossible to achieve but no one faltered, nor fussed, nor complained. Everyone kept working till the job was done, even though many were sick and exhausted. He expanded our vision by helping us to achieve beyond our capacity, teaching us to rely on God's Power not our human power. What a learning experience. We each had the opportunity to bring to our respective nations this expanded **vision and spirit** of working together in harmony to reach and expand our goals so that by His 75th Year Celebration service activities will be growing in the worldwide Sai communities.

In His Discourse that night He said, *"Seva is the best sadhana and makes you see unity in diversity. Recognize the sacredness of society. It is our duty to offer gratitude to the society in which we are born, live and die."*

Let us remember that this Exhibition was dear to the heart of Sai Baba because it showed and told about His Overseas Mission. The photos showed devotees practicing Service, Devotion and Spiritual Education of His children.

The Photos and Books represented "You, the Devotees" giving Him Love by following His Example. Everyone should know that His joy was GREAT as He moved among the exhibits and books!

"Bhagavan Baba inaugurated the Fifth World Conference on November 19th and addressed the Conference on the 20th and 21st. Over 50,000 delegates, seva dal members, and active workers attended the Conference from all parts of India and 90 Overseas Countries." Sanathana Sarathi, December 1990, p. 321.

He said in the November 24th Discourse, *"There are any number of preachers in the world. There are equally numerous scholars. But there are few who practice what they preach and make others do likewise. Here alone there is a power that simultaneously preaches and practices (cheers). Whatever I say, I practice. I speak only on what I am doing. The students present here know this well. Love, love, love. I love all and I ask all to love. My greatest wealth is love. People speak about My powers and My miracles, but My Love is My greatest miracle. All should share in this love. Only then there will be oneness."*

Finally the day we all waited for was there, His Birthday. I arose before dawn and traveled to the Hill View Stadium, because I wanted to avoid the crowds and find a good seat.

"For the lakhs of devotees from all parts of the world gathered in the crowded amphitheater, the entire celebration was an unforgettable experience. The entire atmosphere was surcharged with "Sathyam, Sivam, Sundaram." Everything around was redolent with holiness, from the exquisite Santhi Vedika, from where Bhagavan delivered His discourse; to Vidyagiri, with its imposing 65 foot figure of Hanuman carrying the Sanjiva hill, the inspiring colorful figures of Venugopala, Siva in His yogic pose, Zoroaster proclaiming his great message, Jesus, the very picture of compassion, and the magnificent educational and spiritual edifices all around. Bhagavan who had tirelessly supervised every little detail of the arrangements for the celebrations, conferred His benediction on the lakhs of devotees, who had come from far and near, to have His darshan and listen to his nectarine discourses.

"The entire gathering was thrilled when Bhagavan arrived at the Stadium in His gleaming silver motorized chariot. His arrival was heralded by the firing of shots in adoration, which echoed from all the hills, and by the sudden cascading of water from the top of Vidyagiri to the statue of Siva. It was symbolic of the descent of Ganga from the heavens on to the head of Siva in response to the prayer of Bhagiratha, the famous ancestor of Sri Rama. Bhagavan's arrival was greeted by the chanting of Vedic hymns and the playing of the band by the students of the Sathya Sai Institute. Sanathana Sarathi December 1990, p. 309

In Swami's Birthday discourse He told us of His decision to establish a large hospital here. Because of this profound message, I will quote from the Birthday Discourse in the Sanathana Sarathi, December 1990, p. 314. (see photo)

"We decided to set up a hundred-crore hospital near Prasanthi Nilayam itself (cheers). Even as higher education is free here, "Higher medicine" also will be free. People spend some lakhs to get heart surgery done in the U.S. What is the plight of the poor? Who looks after them? If they go to the cities, they will not get even colored water (mixtures). Recognizing this fact, we have launched this big hospital project. Whether it is heart bypass operation, or a kidney transplant, or a lung operation or brain surgery, everything will be done free (cheers). This has been decided upon from the very starting of the project. The hospital will be opened on November 22, 1991 (cheers).

The first open heart surgery was performed on November 22, 1991. Sai Baba knew it would happen, and He made non-believers believe in His word.

BOOK RELEASED

Shortly, after we arrived home, our new grandson was born, Christian Sathya Bruce, April 3, 1991. What a wonderful gift it was to be there with the children for this exciting event. When Swami said, *"Yes, I will Bless,"* we never dreamed that we would be holding the "blessing" nine months later. Our new grandson was very beautiful.

Since we were gone from the Lake condominium for 10 months the chores and mail stacked up. Just opening 10 months of mail took a week of reading and sorting in between the more pressing chores. It took about a month to catch up on our rest and work.

A couple we knew years ago, resurfaced into our lives. When we arrived home from India we heard that they were attending the Sai Baba Center. Some years earlier when we were new devotees we tried to awaken their interest in Sai Baba, but it did not happen. A keen example of God's Will; not ours.

197

They were anxious to join us on our next trip to India. We mutually decided to go for Christmas. They could spend one month in India. I remember discussing with Robert that perhaps it would be better if they arrived a week later than us. It would give me time to prepare the room, and they would avoid the discomfort of getting the room cleaned and set up. Robert replied, "No, I think they will enjoy experiencing the preparation, as well."

Experience, experience, experience, our Lord Sai tells us.... and what an experience He had waiting for us! The door to the kitchen where we stored our gear had a large funny looking brown cone hanging from it and the door was bumpy and sounded hollow in sections. I had never seen this before! What is it I inquired? The luggage boys were rattling in their native tongue back and forth. Their excitement alerted me to a problem. They knocked the cone down and we saw little white worms crawling everywhere in the wood dust, termites. I exclaimed, "Not termites, Swami! I just got new kitchen cabinets 6 months ago. What surprise is hiding behind the kitchen door?"

Swami tells us, *"When the senses come in contact with sense objects, they can give rise to immense pleasure as well as endless pain."* Indian Culture & Spirituality, P. 57

I was almost afraid to look. It took us nine months to get these kitchen cabinets purchased, installed, and corrected. They finally were completed shortly before we left for home, after months of problems and delays. Now, I stood there wondering if they still **stood** there! Swami says, *"Be prepared for the unexpected."*

Well, the cabinets stood, but not free of termites. It was a nasty job, some of the cabinets had to be removed and taken outside and scrubbed with bleach. We weren't sure at first if they could be saved, but later realized the condition was not as bad as we thought.

All our belongings inside and outside of the cabinets had to be removed from the kitchen and were deposited throughout the apartment. Besides we had groceries from Bangalore and suitcases from home.

I wondered how did we acquire so much "stuff" in one year? Then I remembered many devotees last year coming to my door saying, "We're leaving would you want this?" "Yes, if I can't use it someone else will," I'd say. I had a slogan, "If you can't find it at the Bruce's, it's not at Puttaparthi." Well the slogan just changed to, "It's in Puttaparthi, at the Bruces, but you can't find it!"

There was so much stuff, tables, bedding, dishes, clothes, computers, books etc. inside the apartment that Marian and Dave, had to sit outside, until we could sort and stack some of it making room for us to sleep that night. I recalled Robert's statement months ago.... "it's good for them to experience everything at Prasanthi." This was indeed more than any of us had bargained for.

I vowed to keep only what was necessary and distribute the excessive goods to the village people.

Sai Baba would call this a great beginning for our trip because this experience gives us many opportunities for promotions, *not tests,* He tells us, *promotions.* The first opportunity we had was anger control because of no pest control, then came patience, perseverance, detachment, surrender and exhaustion, I closed my eyes that night thinking "Welcome home, Rita."

After our first darshan, my dear friend Catherine who lives at Prasanthi, caught sight of me and gave me a big hug.

She said jubilantly, "Your book is selling like HOT CAKES at the book store."

Puzzled I asked, "My book is selling in the bookstore?

"Yes," said Catherine.

"In Swami's book store?" I asked.

"Yes," said Catherine. Now I was beginning to get excited.

"When did this happen?" I inquired.

She answered, "Baba released it at His Birthday, and I'm so glad that Our Dear Swami allowed me to be the one to tell you."

As we hugged again the tears of joy swelled in my eyes. It was just perfect! Not one thing could have made this moment any more magnificent. His Divine Love is flawless....

I remembered what a long journey it had been that led up to this exact moment and I knew it, as I felt the relief of completion. The mind can examine our past, touching briefly on thoughts and feelings with amazing speed. In a gestalt pattern I experienced the many events that contributed to the birth of "Vision of Sai." I was feeling a sense of well-being.

The book was delivered to Sai Baba last March. Spring and Summer came and went, the Fall as well, with no news of the book being sold. I finally surrendered to His Will. Now, He has again taken me completely by SURPRISE. That's the second surprise in two days! The termites were not too pleasant but nevertheless a surprise.

Sai teaches us to regard the twin poles of joy and grief, good and bad as equal. He teaches us not to react to either, to treat each with equanimity. All I can say is that I treated them both with equal EXCITEMENT!

Baba says, *"The sun teaches us that when one is oneself, there will be no exhaustion or elation, no disgust or pride. The task of the sun is not something imposed from outside and taken up under compulsion. That is why it performs (its task) systematically and smoothly."* Sathya Sai Newsletter, Spring 92 p. 1

Rose, a dear Aussie friend, said, "Move over, Catherine, it's my time for a hug."

And as we embraced she said, "Your book is so wonderful, I cried while reading it. Everyone likes it!"

I had often wondered how the book would be accepted because of my being so candid. To my astonishment this is what was drawing people to it. Devotees would share with me that they too had similar experiences and could relate to my story. Their heartfelt sharing was giving me a feeling of great satisfaction.

Baba had taught me through the preparation of this book that I must have self-confidence, which simply means confidence in God because He is the Doer. Now, that the work was done I was so grateful that He was allowing me to feel satisfaction.

Swami says, *"First of all, develop self-confidence and that in turn will give you self-satisfaction. Without self-satisfaction, you cannot have contentment. Once you have gained self-satisfaction, then automatically you will be ready for self-sacrifice. Needless to say, where there is self-sacrifice, there will be Self-realization naturally."* Indian Culture & Spirituality p. 171

Because He is a Master Teacher, a Patient Sculptor, and an Artist that stroked me with His brush of Gentle Love, I was able to go beyond what I thought were my human limitations. He taught me to lean heavily on the God within. Daily, my trust improved. The more I learned to "let go" of the doubts and fears of the ego-self; the more Swami came forth.

Swami says that, *"Highly talented persons in different walks of life have not acquired their skills from somewhere outside. All these are but manifestations of their own innate potentialities. It is sheer ignorance to think that any person can be developed by some other person. Everything is in you alone. All that you do by way of your effort is to manifest or give an outer expression to what is already inherent in you."* Indian Culture & Spirituality, p. 135

This day of Sai recognition reached the summit when Robert took me to the book store and in the window under "New Arrivals" was displayed "Vision of Sai". I will always remember that in pleasing the Lord, He returned His love and allowed me to experience great joy and happiness. Swami says, *"Elevate yourself by your own effort."* Indian Culture & Spirituality, p. 127

I also realized that if the book had been sold in the Spring, Summer or Fall... I would not have been here at all. It is His Divine Glory, His Divine Wisdom, and His Divine Love that allowed me to participate in this celebration.

As we were lining up for afternoon darshan, a Seva-Dal reached out and seated me in the beginning of a row, and my friend right behind me. What followed was one of His delightful *leela's*.

We were seated in rows and the first person in each row picks a number or chit for the entire row. This number you pick determines the sequence of your entering the darshan grounds. Since it was the Christmas season, the number of visitors was large and each chit must serve two rows instead of one. The Seva-Dal counted the rows wrongly and allowed the lady in the row before me to select a chit instead of myself. When she realized her mistake, she moved her chit in front of me. It was chit number twelve.

I asked if I could please select my own chit. She replied, "No, if you draw a small number you will feel good, but if you select a larger number you will blame me." I assured her that I would not blame her. I only wanted a chance to draw a new number. The results were Swami's. She then consented and held the chit bag open.

I slid my hand inside and drew out a chit. It was number one! The devotees next to me exclaimed, "It's number one." The Seva-Dal was disappointed at their behavior, yelling in the darshan is not "darshan dharma", but the people were excited! She picked up my chit and said, "You cannot have number one because you are too noisy."

I stayed quiet. The job of being a Seva-Dal at Prasanthi is tough, especially during festival time. There are many people coming to see Our Dear Lord and even between festivals the numbers increase more and more every year. I can certainly understand the need for discipline.

A few minutes later, she returned with the chit and said, "You did not make the noise, therefore your row could go." But she warned all of us of Swami's Will. He wants us to maintain silence. I told my friend to stick next to me like we were glued. The chance of being one and two in the darshan grounds, well there just is no better. We walked fast to secure the first and second seats, next to the old ladies, in front of the Mandir. As we sat, I breathed a sigh of relief.

During darshan Swami came near and took our notes. I spoke, "Thank you for the book, Swami." He stopped and allowed me to have His Padnamaskar. Inside I said, "Oh Swami, how good it is to be home again with you. To be close to the Sweetness of Your Love, to feel the Softness of Your Feet, to see the Bliss that Shines from Your Eyes that pulls me into Your Compassionate, Comforting Being."

At Summer Showers Swami said, *"You are highly fortunate. Even though there are several billions of people in the world, is it not your exceedingly good luck that only you, who are but a few hundreds in number, have been able to get the benefit of this golden opportunity?"* Indian Culture & Spirituality, p. 170

March 10, 1994 Mahasivarathri

SPIRITUAL WORKSHOP

"MERRY CHRISTMAS. All who come embodied are Avatars, that is to say, advents of the Divine, Manifestations of God. What then, is the special feature of Rama, Krishna, Buddha, Christ? Why do you celebrate their Birthdays with such reverential enthusiasm? The speciality is this: they are Aware; you are unaware of the Atma which is Truth. Awareness confers Liberation from bounds, from time, space and causation, from sleep, dream and wakefulness. For you, sleep is fiction, dream is fantasy and wakefulness a many directional storm. Avatars are ever alert, aware, alight. Today is the Birthday of Jesus, celebrated amidst December snowfalls with lights and Christmas trees and prayers." Thought For The Day - December 25, 1991

In mid-December, the Christmas and Satsang Program was just beginning. Sai devotee's from every nation were arriving minute by minute. Every available space was being occupied. The Christmas fever and fervor was gathering momentum. I felt tired because of the jet lag and extra work with the termites so I decided to rest and not go to satsang this particular morning.

When Robert returned he said, "Something interesting happened this morning." I said, "What?" He replied, "Your name was announced by the Christmas Committee Chairman, to be a Co co-ordinator of the Christmas Play with the Author of the play." "My name? How can that be, I wasn't asked? This is not the usual method." Another surprise!

I inquired inside, 'Swami, what's this about?' I heard Him say, "If you were asked would you have accepted?"

My thoughts replied "NO, I wouldn't accept because I've never co-ordinated a play or a project of this magnitude." The voice inside replied, "That's why you were not asked!" I prayed that He give me a sign that this was His Will.

The next morning when I was walking to darshan, my eyes were cast to the ground. Suddenly, a women brushed quickly in front of me. I noticed we had the same colored sari, as I raised my eyes I noticed the same colored shawl. Then I saw that it was the devotee that had directed the Christmas Play for many years. The voice inside said, "You are walking in her foot steps."

As I sat for darshan, I thought about this experience. 'With 30,000 devotees at Prasanthi, You had the devotee who directed Your Christmas Play for years walk directly in front of me, wearing the same colored clothes. The circumstances are surely unusual, especially since I prayed for a sign.' I thought if Sai was asking me to help, how could I refuse? I knew it would be a good learning experience for me.

After darshan, I asked Robert for his intuitive opinion. He replied, "I think it would be a great learning experience. You need to interact with the devotees who live here because you too are living here. It would be nice to know them better, plus the chance to know devotees from all over the world."

Why am I including this story in my book? Because there may be some of you who have been or will be asked to take on a leadership role in the future for Sai

Baba's Organization. I have through many mistakes, learned what not to do.... but this time Dear Baba clearly taught me what to do. Perhaps it will help you.

I have been in the Organization for many years and the road has not been easy. In fact there have been some real hair raising experiences. If you are a devotee, you certainly can identify with this statement because Swami has only one interest and that is the removal of our ego, so His Divine Love can flow through us. He combines impossible personalities to work together and of course this is a sure method of ego rubbing and sometimes sparks fly in the process.

The song title "Blood, Sweat, and Tears" took on a new meaning after I became a devotee of Swami's. When we sacrifice our ego; we shed Blood, Sweat is the hard work it takes to play the game, and Tears release and clean the emotions. Thank God for the Grace of tears.

One day Swami gave me a wonderful description of the purpose for His Organization, I wrote...... "Sai Baba's Organization is a medium that Swami uses, not only, for the purpose of helping Society at large, but it is first a medium that He uses to mold and develop the ego-lessness of each member. Over the years of development, it sometimes appears as if the Organization has stood still. Not so, many individual egos are being reshaped. changing egos is a subjective move; they are not measured by tangible means. This expansive measure of progress can only be envisioned by God. But collectively, the reshaping of individual members' character is a giant step forward.

"Don't lose hope, measurable progress will happen. When God's army of devotees are armed with faith, humility, love of all beings, and selfless service to God, "VICTORY" will be society's halo!"

Many times I wanted to quit and came within a whisker of doing so. But one day when I was absolutely finished, I wrote a letter to Swami telling Him the reason I was leaving His Organization. As I was writing, these words came from within:

"There are two kinds of devotees doing service. Some are working for themselves; some are working for me. Do not replace their "ego actions" with your ego wanting "recognition." You are working for Me, you must expect these tests often. It is to teach you that pain and joy must be treated equally.

"You must be the voice to accomplish what I wish to accomplish. **If all the good people leave the organization, what will become of My Mission?** Then evil will have no restraint. Speak for me, Rita; not for Rita. The concern for all Sai devotees should be: Is Swami's work being blocked or stopped? And how can it continue? I want solutions, not resolutions!" (Action not lip service.)

I stopped writing. "If the good people leave the organization than what will become of My Mission?" Oh Swami, you could have said anything but those words. You truly know my heart and how to get me to respond. From that day, I have never considered leaving again, no matter how rough the road becomes.

Sai Baba announced at the Fifth World Conference in November 1991 the following: *"Embodiments of the Divine Atma, take a vow to develop the Sai Organization day by day. Take all people within the fold. People who have gone away from the organization are the unfortunate ones; you should not become unfortunate. Come what may, do not give up this Organization. Consider this Organization as your life's breath. This is a real service. This is real penance. Take a vow on these lines to become experts. This is what I desire. Swami will be with you in whatever you are doing."* Sathya Sai Newsletter Fall 1992, p. 11

What I was about to experience would help me in my future Sai Organizational work, or for that matter in all my relationships with people.

I felt so incompetent because I had never coordinated a project of this size before. We had one week to get a script, design costumes, scenes, cast and direct a large number of children. They had fifty last year. My heart sank, 'Oh Swami, I'm feeling so inadequate.'

Then I caught myself. 'Who is this I?' If I think that Rita is the doer then I will be identifying with the body and its personality. I received the following message from my inner voice:

"Nothing that happens in your life is coincidental, every moment, every detail is in fact planned, energized and acted through you by me. I am the DOER. You are the instrument. God can create positive or negative actions through you. If your ego has a flaw, I will bring it forth for you to witness. How else can you be purified? If a flaw is not seen or detected; it cannot be polished out.

209

I am the flaw, the polisher and the gemstone. Your ego is worthless, without My presence. It does not exist. Therefore any thought, word or deed done by you cannot be claimed or acclaimed by you.

"Henceforth remember, you are not great or important because of an action nor are you faulty or negligent because of an action... everything in this Universe is me! Realize that it is I that is the **doer**; not you."

Swami says, *"Embodiments of the Divine Spirit, realize that you are not this body, this mind, this intellect or this intelligence. You are embodiments of the Divine. Concentrate on your efforts to realize the Divine. There is nothing that cannot be achieved by sincere learning and continuous practice.*

I wanted all of us who worked on the Christmas Play to give Swami for Christmas a Gift of Love by conducting ourselves as examples of Love in Action. I remembered my previous experience here working with the 65h Birthday Book and Photo Exhibit Committee. Baba was so happy with us and showered us with His Love. I treasured that experience of working together in the spirit of love and harmony, and how I wanted to re-create the same atmosphere!

Each year Our Dear Mother and Father Sai Baba invites all His children to come home to Prasanthi to celebrate the Birthday of His Son, Jesus Christ. A Divine Birthday Party at Puttaparthi! I can only imagine if I were having all these children home for a week at Christmas, I would want to keep them very busy. It appears the same with the Lord.

If you were looking down from the clouds over Prasanthi you would see He has His children busy with a variety of group activities: choir practice, musicians rehearsals, canteen workers, seva dal workers, play writers, directors, children helpers, costume designers, prop workshops, decorating, food preparation etc., etc.

Sai says, *"Forget all else and stick to the orders that I give you; I want only to initiate you into the spiritual path of love and service. Do not be ashamed that you have been asked to watch a heap of sandals, or carry water to the thirsty or stand at the gate. The privilege and pleasure consists of the way in which you use your skill and time for helping others. So, you long to serve me; let me tell you this, serving those who serve me gives me as much satisfaction as if you were serving me. Serving anyone is serving me, for I am in all."* Sathya Sai Newsletter Spring 1992, p. 21

The greatness of His strategy is that the entire work in each group centers around God. We are practicing God Consciousness. He keeps our thoughts, words, and deeds focused on the Divine. The festival celebrations are really Intense Spiritual Training Workshops. It is intense because what would normally take months of preparation to reach completion; He reduced into a week. The greater the force of emotional experience; the deeper the remembrance.

The Overture taught is: ***"LOVE ALL; SERVE ALL."***

Swami says, *"Love means Service, which means Spiritual discipline, which means Expansion, self-enlargement, reaching out to the very horizon of being and becoming! - until all is I."* Seva, A Flower at His Feet, p. 50

211

The Christmas Festival is a fertile environment for the overseas devotees for practicing Sai Baba's teachings on service.

Just about the time I was becoming more comfortable with the idea of this leadership role, the author resigned as coordinator with me. She wanted to work with the creative aspect of the play; not the administrative. He was gently pulling the rug a little further out from beneath me.

Robert was Treasurer last year and asked to be again, so we both attended the first Christmas Committee meeting. It was decided that I select a control committee.

The first priority was the manuscript. The play needed to be edited and a devotee who by profession was a screen play editor volunteered to help. The director, author, and screen play editor went to work on the manuscript. I had hoped that we would have a rough draft by the next day.

These three were on the control committee, along with a devotee who has lived in Prasanthi for years and worked on the Christmas Play for many years. I called her my consultant.

When I awoke the next morning and got up my hip joint snapped out of place. It was painful and I could not go to darshan. I said, "Swami! What is going on? How can I work on the play if I cannot walk?" As the day's events unfolded it seemed that He didn't want me to leave and made sure I was confined to the room.

Directly after darshan there was a knock on my door.

It was my consultant bringing me the news of the days 'challenges.' It seems that the play did not get edited, yesterday and the screen-play editor had gone to Bangalore. The person incharge of costumes had quit, and the play director believed in "Open Theater" meaning no props or backdrops. All presenting serious problems to my consultant.

Since she had years of experience and understood time management and the logistics of presenting a play in the Poornachandra Hall that accommodated 30,000 devotees, she was concerned by these over-night developments. I listened to her advice. Thank God I had her; she taught me so much.

She had two main concerns. First no script. Without a play nothing could begin. We had parents, children, singers, costume designers, prop people, all standing by.... waiting. If we didn't keep them busy, we risked losing them.

Sai Baba told a devotee to carry a first aid box, while helping others. He said, *"Carry in it a few tablets of discrimination and detachment, an ounce or two of sense control, a packet of love and a bandage strip of fortitude. Only then can you effectively render first aid to people suffering from a stroke of ego, or a bout of greed, or jaundiced vision, or an allergy to serving others."*

The director gathered the children and used this time by having them do dramatic floor exercises. He was teaching the children how to take orders and perform them. I watched him play and work with the children. It was magic to see his love bring the best out of them.

213

These preliminary activities helped him to become acquainted with the children and select the one best suited for a particular role.

I told my consultant to get the author and we would work on the play in my room. We had a computer and we could edit it there. The play had some Shakespearean verse. The play was grand but too long and complex to accomplish in one week and fit into the 40 minute time slot that Swami had given us. My role was beginning to take form.

I was concerned to accept this position of leadership because I had no experience in "plays." But Swami was clearly showing me that to accept leadership, we do not need to be Ph.D.'s or experts, only **Sai Devotees**. Swami sent me the experts, qualified people, all I needed to do was to stay centered and help them to work in harmony for the good of all. I was there to serve them in any way possible, interfere only when absolutely necessary and above all else remember that He is the DOER!

Sai says, *"Help as much as you can, as efficiently as you can, as silently as you can, as lovingly as you can; leave the rest to God, who gave you the chance to serve."*

The author came with my consultant, we spent nearly eight hours in my room working on the play. The re-writing of another person's creation is a sensitive situation. We did not want to hurt the author's feelings. It took time working with her as we tried to understand her concept and the message that she wanted to express in this play. It was not easy, and we all had to give something of ourselves.

214

It was late, when a friend who later became the Secretary for the play director walked into my room at the exact moment that we needed someone to type a rough draft of the play. It was finished just in time for the 7:30 p.m. Christmas Committee Meeting, when they had to approve the play.

We presented the play and it was approved. After the meeting I stood up and there came a noise from my body. The woman next to me said, "What was that?" I replied, "My hip joint just snapped back into place."

Twelve hours ago, I awoke with it going out. He made sure I stayed in the room that day and helped with the play. My hip has never done that before nor since. Isn't He funny! But He is also letting me know that He is ever Present.

Next we worked together with the Director who was excellent with children. He wanted no props or backdrops on stage because He wanted nothing to distract from the children. A beautiful thought.

But we also needed to address the logistics of a play in the Poornachandra Hall. Because of the distance between the stage and the back of the Hall, without a backdrop or props the people in the back, many of them local villagers, would not see the children acting as props, e.g. instead of houses, two children holding their hands together to form the frame of a house with some sort of costume. We needed some visual communication also, because many in the audience did not understand English.

215

Again, the situation called for co-operation. I named it ego-operation! We compromised and had some props and some open theatre. It was a good combination of the artistic and practical.

I recalled Sai Baba's words. *"Hurt never; help ever."* He says, *"If you hurt others, they will hurt you in retaliation. This kind of reaction, resound and reflection are inherent in man's mind. Hence you should scrupulously follow the maxim: 'Hurt never; help ever.'*

It didn't make any great difference if a line in the script was misplaced or the color of a costume was one shade and not another, even though our ego thinks it's so important at the time. I continually repeated that all our desires must be sacrificed inorder to give a Gift of Love to Swami at Christmas. The most important aspect of this exercise was for us to unite, not fight!

Costumes became the next agenda. We had another lady volunteer to be incharge, but we needed costume designs. Time was the pressing factor. A call to Our Lord Baba for help and He replied by sending us a fashion illustrator! Just as before he sent an expert. This woman devotee was so talented. She completed all the costume sketches in a few hours. They were magnificent. He is the Doer!

The costume team did an exceptional job. The woman in charge followed Swami's Ceiling on Desires program, one rule is *"Don't waste money."* The costume group re-made and re-used costumes and materials from previous years. They excelled in saving a good sum of money and the costumes were anything but shabby. Instead they were exceptionally brilliant and creative.

As I observed Swami viewing the play, the costumes of the sheep and donkey seemed to amuse Him. The sheep costumes were made out of cotton wool and the little children moving like sheep tickled the audience. The donkey costume was another hit. They created a two man donkey costume for Mary to sit upon as they entered Bethlehem, very professional.

This group also had their moments of challenges from Swami. He didn't miss a person nor an opportunity. Last year they had 50 children and this year we had a record of 92! The number had almost doubled. This meant 92 costumes to be made in a week!

On December 23, we realized that the Director had assigned many children with two different roles. This would demand costume changes and there was neither a place nor time for costume changes. It took an entire day, to straighten out what child was playing what role and in what costume!

We actually had 80 children between the ages of 5 and 14. The additional twelve were 'itsy bitsys' under the age of 5 years. This was the first year they were included. The volunteers promised to coach them and take full responsibility before, during and after the performance. They were so organized and pleaded for the children to participate. Their sweetness overcame my logic. I thought at this point, "What is a few more!"

They stole the show on several occasions and I saw Swami chuckle when they were on stage.

The little boys were dressed as bunny rabbits, hopping on stage with large orange felt carrots in their mouths. The carrots were place at the feet of Jesus in the manger. The girls were flowers. Dressed in green stems with large felt flower hats. They stood beside the manger.

We had an Advent scene in the play where the children were required to walk with candles but real candles were too dangerous. We presented the problem to the prop-group and they made long candles with light bulbs, that worked on batteries. I was told that one day when Swami came to visit the play practice back stage, He took the candle prop completely apart. He asked the prop people to make 40 of them for His students. During the play the lights waving in the dark was really dramatic.

The director who was very imaginative had a "Walking Table." There was a Christmas Morning scene showing a Sai devotee family. The Christmas tree was lit, the fireplace held stockings with pictures of Sai Baba and Jesus above. It was Christmas morning and the children came rushing down for breakfast.... and started fighting. The table got mad and walked away. Swami chuckled! The father told the children that Sai Baba tell us to *"Watch our Thoughts, Words, and Actions"* because they affect everything.

Communication was important for the success of the play. When I work with devotees in the Sai Organization, I remember how important it is to share our ideas and Sai's Ideals. We not only need to communicate our suggestions in a thoughtful manner but we need to remind each other of Sai's Teachings. This can quickly center everyone to the real purpose of our job.

Baba, *"I must say plainly that ninety out of a hundred among you have not clearly visualized the purpose for which I have allowed you to form these organizations...It is to build upon the earth the fatherhood of God and the brotherhood of men on strong foundations. This must be clearly grasped by all of you. You are not engaged in social service through these organizations; you are engaged in your own service. All the items of work are aimed at expanding your heart and purifying it.* Sathya Sai Speaks VI, p. 321

Each night in my room after darshan, we held a meeting to discuss the next days work schedule and talk about our agreements and disagreements. I've heard Swami say, *"You cannot always oblige; but you can always speak obligingly."* Discourse Kodaikanal April 1992

Besides all the normal problems you encounter in the production of a play that is pressed into a very tight schedule, the Lord has another hidden agenda. This unseen element is Sai Baba's washing machine! It is wise for us to remember when we work with fellow devotees, that He is cleansing us. He creates circumstances that can provoke old hurts, personality weakness, old programming, etc., etc.

For example; if you are prompt and organized; He could have you work with someone who is late and un-organized. If you have a strong personality; He may surround you with very sensitive personalities. If you get angry; He can match you with unreasonable behavior. If you had an authoritarian Father; He could give you the same type of personality to work with. If you have been dominated by a mother; you may be working with a domineering person. If you are tired and sick; He can give you such a responsible position that you must continue to work. If you get irritable under stress; He may give you stress. He creates countless situations for each of us to look at ourselves and our egos. The very nature of this cleansing calls for great sensitivity on the part of all devotees.

The success of this play depended upon each participant sacrificing their time, comfort, or desire, for the unity of the whole. Their dedication and devotion to Sai Baba was an inspiration to me. Whenever there was an opportunity, I thanked the devotees and encouraged their labor of Love.

Being a member of the Sai Organization under the leadership of Our Lord Sai Baba whose goal is nothing short of Self-Realization is distinctly different from belonging to a social organization.

Swami says, *"There are thousands of organizations already working with such aims, but what is the special need for an organization bearing my name? You must realize me in all, and serve all in a spirit of worshipful dedication.* Sathya Sai Speaks 6, p. 323-324

The children rehearsed in-between darshan and bhajans, about eight hours a day. The volunteers worked continuously, coaching and occupying the children. Eighty children confined to the Poornachandra Hall most of the day was an overwhelming task. The volunteers also had to arrange seating for all these children back stage before the play commenced and they had to keep absolute silence because Swami would be there. This required the volunteers to enforce discipline, and stress to the children the importance of remaining silent and sitting still.

The foreign children are not used to sitting quietly. They are used to a high level of stimulation and had to cope with sitting quietly and silently. Most children are a bundle of jitters, if it's not their mouth moving it's their bodies. The children were being taught self-control, and so were we.... even though there were times we felt like shouting to get their attention. So we too were having many chances to excel in self-control.... Swami's Spiritual Training Program did not exempt the children, they too were learning.

Sai says, *"Generally, I speak sweetly, but on this matter of discipline, I will not grant any concessions... I will insist on strict obedience. I shall not reduce the rigor to suit your level, for that will only ruin you. I pay attention to your ultimate good."* Sathya Sai Speaks 2, p. 186

The make-up committee requested make-up and devotees supplied it from every country. The make-up artists had to practice matching the correct face with every character. The children really seemed to enjoy their faces being different.

Dress rehearsal took **team** work. We were assigned a hall which replaced the backstage dressing room. The costume group plus volunteers, pressed clothes and dressed each child. The make-up group did their faces and the volunteers tried to keep the children calm. Patience was the word for the day!

The director had the awesome job, a gigantic responsibility to make it work! The large number of children is what made this particular Christmas Play a "New Challenge!" The timing was essential; moving people, moving props, synchronizing the voice reader with each child's action on stage, cueing the musicians and the choir. "Let the Play begin," said the Director!

The time had come, the work had been done and now the performance was in the hand of Our Master Director, Sathya Sai Baba.

They moved Swami's chair to the designated spot, amongst the men. Robert was Blessed to sit in front of Sai and I had an aisle seat on the ladies side, across from Baba. How fortunate we both were. I had an excellent seat to observe Swami, as He watched the play. His eyes never left the stage, He laughed and smiled as if He was seeing it for the first time!

Baba tells us, *"Everything given to God by the devotee was first given to the devotee by God."* Kodaikanal April 1992

The children performed as professionals! I could hardly believe that this was the same group, I had watched practicing. They were excellent. The color of the set, costumes, make-up and lighting dramatized what we did not see in the day light, as we practiced.

When the play was over, Robert said to Swami,

222

"Picture with the Children, Baba?" Swami paused, then leaned forward and said to Robert, *"Play over?"* "Yes, Swami," replied Robert. *"Play over"* repeated Swami. "Yes" said Robert. It appeared that Baba did not want it to end.

Swami got up and was pleased. He joined the children on stage for the pictures, and when He went back stage He told the workers: *"Very happy, very happy!"*

The children were happy, their parents were happy, the workers were happy, because they made Our Lord happy! It was not a Merry Christmas but a Happy Christmas.

Swami's love had melted our hearts and the days of labor and exhaustion even tasted sweet. As I walked home, I spoke with some of the play workers, they were so joyful and full of smiles. Sai Baba says, *"All I want is your love."* They gave their best.

There are times that Our Lord Sathya Sai calls on us to reach out and expand our capacity beyond what we think are our limits. Therein lies the "quirk" our limit is ego. We are thinking of the individual as doer; not the Divine. The Sai Devotee does not forget that a pure heart is the greatest requirement for any role that the Lord gives us. If our heart is pure, than only His Divine Wisdom moves our actions; instead of the individual ego.

The following is an excerpt from a discourse given by Sai Baba on November 21, 1986.

SELFLESS SERVICE

"It is necessary for us to know why terrible, atrocious actions are committed in the world. It is basically because we are not giving selfless service filled with love, and therefore all sorts of (wrong) desires have developed in people.

Embodiments of divine love! We should not waste even a fraction of a second of valuable time. Man has forgotten the significance of divine love to which he is entitled, because he is not thinking along proper lines. Man is wasting time, indulging in talk, claiming to do things which make no sense.

Service may be compared to a sharp sword. When such a powerful instrument is in the hands of people who know how to handle it properly, it can bring tremendous good, but if it is in the hands of someone who does not know how to use it, it can cause great harm. How should one make use of the sword? The same question applies to our actions. How should we make use of our power to act? Only people who have made an analysis (of their situation) should undertake action. People who undertake work without knowing the secret of work (action) spoil the sanctity of action. It is in this context that we have to make self-inquiry to find out if we have the requisites and qualifications to understand selfless service. The important qualifications are compassion, humility, and courage. Only those who have these qualities can be examples to the world. A person who is given to egoism, ostentatious behavior, and attachment can never undertake selfless service and expect to perform it well.

Man gives up his "human nature" because of egoism. Because of a showy nature and ostentatious behavior, he becomes artificial in his actions. Because of attachment, he develops animal qualities and animal feelings. He cannot develop confidence in himself with these characteristics. A person who has such doubts can never have faith in himself.

One who does not believe in himself cannot trust others. A person who has neither faith in himself nor belief in others cannot undertake selfless service in society. Therefore, in the first instance, egoism must be destroyed; only then can one develop humility. Only a person who has humility has the authority to undertake social work. Then they must put an end to showy or ostentatious behavior. They should remove attachment also. One has to recognize that the same Divinity exists in every human being; and then, with that unifying feeling, he can undertake selfless service in the community. Without becoming a servant, one can never become a good leader.

Today the world has come to such a chaotic condition because people, who do not know how to serve others, have become leaders. From time immemorial, there have been millions of people who have undertaken work, sacrificing everything to serve others. But gradually, the number of such people who are willing to sacrifice, is dwindling. People who know how to serve have become rare. In the name of "service to others," they are deceiving themselves. Only such actions can be called service which are performed while forgetting one's self entirely and recognizing the Divinity existing everywhere and in everyone. There are people who are helpless with no one to look after them. Undertaking activities which would help them is very important, but we must remember to correct our own character and qualities. We have to recognize the importance of morality and truth. We should be prepared to sacrifice anything for the sake of the country. When I say country, it does not signify "mud" but people. We have to feel that service to humanity is service to God. Patience and perseverance are important. Among all vows, telling the truth and having good character are the greatest. In fact, honor is greater than life itself. But today we have become absolutely imitative. We act as if we are artificial in our nature. We have become like an elephant which does not know its own extraordinary strength.

By big speeches and high-sounding words, we are trying to preach to others. However, this is not going to save us. We have to put an end to the kind of preaching which is not supported by any practice. By speeches which are memorized from texts, we are not going to transform the world. We have to enter into activities with total simplicity and selflessness, doing silent and unselfish work. We need to practice, and then we can undertake preaching to others. Practicing is far more precious than talking. Words may bring temporary satisfaction, but gradually that strength will leave the body. By proper practice, we can bring about transformation in the world.

Whatever Swami has said is in the best interest of all. We'll have to take this in that spirit. Forget the past mistakes and undertake service activities, keeping in view all that Swami has said. In the future, sanctify your lives."

SERVICE SAI ORGANIZATION

DIVINE DISCOURSE

What are the reasons for the treacherous, cruel acts in this world? They are: the decline of selfless service, the increase of meaningless feelings, and the multiplication of senseless desires. Follow the path of the birds that fly in the sky with the help of their wings. Make love and service your two wings, and fly in the sky like the bird that will enable you to reach the goal faster.

Embodiments of Divine Love! Only selfless service will encourage man to reach the higher state of humanity. Selfless service alone gives the needed strength and courage to awaken the sleeping humanity in man. Just duty alone is not enough for the progress of humankind. Love, kindness, morality, honesty, compassion, and forgiveness are very essential factors. Without these qualities, man cannot perform selfless service.

227

The root causes of pain and pleasure, love and hate, and materialistic desires are the temptations of the mind. "This is mine; that is thine." These dual feelings are the sole reasons for the desires or temptations of the mind. The reason for this dualism is selfishness. Man has become so selfish that he does not care for others, or anything other than his own welfare. The main reason for these dual feelings of love and hatred is selfishness.

One who constantly thinks of his own body, his own family, his own wealth, and his own comfort is a truly selfish man. The only way to cleanse such a hardhearted man is through service to humanity. It is necessary to recognize that a man's life is meant to be spent in selfless service, and in the service of the Self. Such a life of service is not to gain either name or fame, to allow expression of one's ego, or in the furtherance of one's own ends. Service which is done for selfish gain is not service at all.

The inability to identify the sanctity and divinity of service is what holds man back from a life of service. Therefore, service to humanity should be understood to be service to the Self, not merely service to society. Society does not need your service, unless you realize that such service is indeed for your own spiritual good, not for the gratification of the ego.

A life which is not spent in service is a life of darkness. Understand that society is the source of whatever pleasure you derive and whatever pleasure you achieve in life. Society and nature are the fountain of your joy, wealth, and enlightenment, and they deserve your service. Just a small instance to illustrate the point: when we drop a handkerchief, and somebody picks it up, we say "thanks." Don't we need to express at least that much gratitude to a sacred and divine society which has given us all these comforts and pleasures?

Service should be our primary responsibility and our main goal. We should not waste our lives in pursuit of useless attractions. Money and materials are not essential for service, but a loving heart is. We should fill our hearts with love.

In nature, consciousness is never wasted. When it is developed with ego, it generates bad deeds, but when it is associated with the Self (Atma), it produces good deeds.

Man is unable to realize the basic fact that it is discrimination which sets him apart from the rest of the animals. He is forgetting his very basic humanity. Today man is physically a human, but he lacks humanity. He is only after materialistic possessions, money, power, authority, physical comforts and pleasures. He thinks that money and wealth are the only way to salvation and happiness. But money and wealth are root causes of destruction. Money is not looking after us; it is not protecting us.

Some money is, of course, essential. But man should be able to lead a meaningful life with just enough or with a limited amount of money. But today, acts of service or, for that matter, any of the deeds of man are filled with show, pride, and ego. As long as you are bound by such qualities as egoism, you cannot understand the nature of Atma (Soul). Without understanding the nature of Atma, humanity will not bloom. If humanity does not blossom, then one cannot be called human at all. One can only be a man in physical form, but not a fully blossomed, realized soul.

Therefore, the main criterion for service is sacrifice. Egoism should be the first quality to be offered for sacrifice. Giving up bad feelings is, in itself, sacrifice, and that sacrifice becomes a man's fortune. Sacrifice does not mean that one should renounce his possessions and his family, and leave the comforts of his home to lead an ascetic life in the forest.

Due to the lack of people who can teach or preach our sacred Indian culture, its important tenets and principles, and their implications, today's society is headed in the wrong direction. It is a misconception to think that we are serving others. We should attain the feeling that we are serving God in the form of others. We should develop the confidence that God is in everyone.

When we blame others, we accumulate the fruits of their sins. This is the law of the universe; because the other individual whom you are blaming is not someone else, but God Himself. Therefore, do not blame or hurt anyone. Doing so only reflects on your own character. It is foolishness to express inhumane qualities. When you point out one mistake in a person, others will be ready to point out ten mistakes in you. When a man realizes this truth, he will not blame others.

It is a typical characteristic of a mean person to boast about himself and to put down others. A man can be called "human" only when he gives up such bad qualities and wicked feelings. We should see God in every form. Only *then the true acts of service will come to fruition, and you can derive joy from them. When we develop the feeling that it is our good fortune to be able to serve others, and when we serve with sanctity, purity, and selflessness, only then can it be called service.*

Embodiments of the divine Atma, you have designated yourselves to perform these service activities to attain divinity or to reach a higher state of consciousness, according to your own levels of devotion. However, there is no relationship between these service activities and Swami. Purity of the heart and mind is right action. Dharma (right action) washes away the filth from the hearts and minds, and only with such purified hearts should you perform your actions. This is what Sai teaches. Any superior actions that we do are only done to cleanse your hearts. If you think that through deeds alone you can attain liberation or a higher state of consciousness, you are wrong. How can you attain the supremacy and sanctity of life without purity of mind? You should develop the feeling that you are performing your deeds to attain purity of heart. You should not encourage the idea that deeds will help to attain the supreme Divinity in life. But, on the other hand you should recognize that your life has been created only to perform such divine, selfless service. From janma (birth) you should do karma (action), karma should lead to dharma (right action), and dharma leads one to Brahman (the Divine, God). That is what janma, karma, dharma, and Brahman are. These four are interrelated.

It is mere weakness to give the silly excuse that you have no time for service because you are so busy with your duties. Cleaning streets in the villages is not the only service available to you. Discharging your duties in a righteous manner is, in itself, a service. One should regard service as performing one's duties properly and working enough to justify the pay one gets. If a person works conscientiously every minute of the day, doing the job that he is hired to do, that is service. Today, however, you can hardly find anyone, from a laborer to an executive, whose work is worth the pay he gets. Employees are always asking for more money, but they never ask whether or not they are working enough for the pay they are already receiving. This is betrayal of a trust. Whose money is this? This is the people's money. If you cheat people in this manner, it is a sin.

When a teacher is teaching his students genuinely and properly, that is service. A businessman need not sweep the streets. If he conducts his business in a moral way, that itself is service. If he does not exploit people for more profits, that is service. When a person has such a selfless feeling, he automatically becomes the "servant." One should lead one's life to one's own mental satisfaction. He should contemplate his behavior to determine whether or not it is up to his satisfaction. You can please Sai only by performing your duties to the fullest, serving society whenever and wherever you get the opportunity. Service is not limited to serving individuals. Serving society is also service. Any action that benefits the country is service. One should experience divinity in the service. For serving, you need not have anybody's shelter, or protection, or advice. Wherever you feel the need, serve. There is no distinction between acts of service. It is immaterial whether you are serving the poor or the rich. You should be able to serve anyone, at any place, and under any circumstances.

Miseries, sorrows, and pain are the same for everyone. That is why you should serve anyone in need without hesitation. In villages people are living in highly unacceptable conditions. We should go to the villages and implant the feeling of service in them by teaching its importance. Many of you are going to villages, cleaning the dirty areas, and coming back. But how long can you do this? Why are we doing this cleaning? Would it not be better to help the villagers understand the importance of cleanliness? If surroundings are not clean, it affects our health and the health of our children. This ill health will ruin our lives. We will not be able to perform our duties. Good health is the best wealth one can have. We should explain the facts about personal hygiene to the villagers so that they can keep their surroundings clean. Going once or twice a month to the villages to clean them is of no use. We should get the villagers to do these things by themselves. This is service.

Similarly, what is the meaning of "Ceiling on Desires?" Man is deluded by his unlimited desires. He is living in a dream world. He is forgetting the Supreme Consciousness. That is why it is important to keep our desires under control, to place a ceiling on them. We are spending too much money. Instead of inordinate spending for our own pleasures, we should be spending for the relief of the poor and needy. This is the real meaning of "Ceiling on Desires." Do not make the mistake of thinking that giving money is all that is needed, however. Do not give to others while allowing your own desires to continue to multiply. Curtail your desires, as materialistic desires lead to a restless and

233

disastrous life. Desires are a prison. Man can be freed only by limiting his wants. You should have desire only for life's bare necessities.

How can you reduce desires? **First, food**. *Eat only what you need to eat. Don't be greedy. Do not take more than you can eat and waste the rest, because wasting food is a great sin. The surplus food can feed another stomach. Do not waste food because food is God, life is God, and man is born from food. Food is the main source of man's life, body, mind, and character. The gross part of the food, which is the major portion of the food consumed by the body, is thrown out as waste matter. A minute amount of the food, which is the subtle part, is assimilated by the body and flows as blood. And a minuscule amount, which is the subtlest part of the food, makes up the mind. Therefore, the mind is the reflection of the food consumed. The reason for the present beastly and demonic tendencies in our minds is because of the food we consume.*

Instead of kindness, compassion, love, and patience, only bad qualities such as hatred and attachment are being perpetrated. Therefore, the quality of the food that we eat should be very pure, very clean, very sanctified and satwic. Man receives real nourishment from such food.

A large part of the water we drink is expelled as urine. A minute part of the water consumed becomes prana (the life force). Therefore, the nature of the food and water that we take in decides our character. Only by controlling the quality of our food and water can we attain divinity. This is why food is said to be God. Hence, to waste food is to waste God. Do not waste food. Eat only what you need, and be sure that what you eat is satwic. Give any surplus food to those in need.

Second, money. Indians consider money or wealth as the goddess Lakshmi. Do not misuse money. By doing so you will only become a slave to bad qualities, bad ideas, and bad habits. Use your money wisely for good deeds. Do not waste money, as misuse of money is evil. It will lead you along the wrong path.

Third, time. The most important, the most needed factor, is time. One should not waste time. Time should be spent in a useful manner. Time should be sanctified because everything in this creation is dependent on time. Even our scriptures say that God is referred to as Time and as Non-time. God is not limited by Time. He is beyond Time; He is Time; He restricts Time. Time is the embodiment of God. Everything depends on Time.

The main reason for man's birth and death is time. Time is the main factor in our growth. If we waste time, our lives will be wasted. Therefore, time is an essential part of our life. Do not degrade time by spending it participating in unnecessary conversations, or by getting involved in others' personal matters. The truth behind the saying "Don't waste time" is that no time should be wasted in evil thoughts and acts. Instead, make use of time in an efficient way.

Fourth, energy. Our physical, mental, and spiritual energies should never be wasted. You might ask me: "How are we wasting our energies?" If you see bad things, your energy is wasted. Hearing bad things, speaking evil, thinking evil thoughts, and doing evil deeds wastes your energy. Conserve your energy in all these five areas, and *make your life more meaningful.*

See no evil-see what is good. Hear no evil-hear what is good. Speak no evil-speak what is good. Think no evil-think what is good. Do no evil-do what is good. This is the path to God.

The path of divinity is not seeing, listening, speaking, thinking, or doing anything bad. If we are not following this path, we are wasting our energy. On account of this waste of energy, we are losing our memory power, intelligence, power of discrimination, and power of justice.

Today's man is not capable of discriminating between good and bad. Then how can he enter the path of right action? You might be wondering how this is possible; how are we wasting time? For example, when you turn on the radio to listen to a certain program, whether you raise or lower the volume of the sound, as long as the radio is on, the current is being used. Our mind is like the radio. Whether you talk with others or only think within yourself, you are consuming energy.

Your mind is working all the time. Since it is always turned on, you are consuming a lot of energy. Instead of wasting that power, energy, or force in mental meandering, isn't it better to spend your time in thinking good thoughts? The Ceiling on Desires Program has been proposed so that man does not waste anything in the areas of food, money, time, or energy.

Today, however, some service-oriented people and workers in the Sri Sathya Sai World Organizations have not fully realized this. Instead they are giving money, thinking that it is service. They are cleverly getting out of serving, while their desires are growing out of bounds. We should gradually try to change these attitudes. The main goal of the Sai Organization is to enable members, workers, and officers to lead ideal, perfect, and happy lives. Therefore, we must live up to the high ideals of the Organization and transform ourselves into ideal beings, thus helping others to follow our example.

Sai Organizations do not discriminate on the basis of nationality, caste, race, or religion.

Embodiments of the Divine, morality is more important than nationality. We should ponder more upon love than religion. What is the use of cultivating religion without love in the heart? Such a religion only contributes to our insanity. We have only one religion: the religion of humanity, and love is our morality. We should prove our ideals to the world. This type of religion and love alone will help man to pave the way to the betterment of mankind.

Since ancient times our country has been preaching truth and right action to mankind. Even now, our traditions echo these injunctions: "Speak only the truth," and "Do only righteous deeds." When such a sacred nation is once again filled with truth and right action, and when kindness, love, and affection become natural, such a nation has genuine prosperity.

If, however, a nation is developed only scientifically, without discrimination, such development is wasted. One good hearted person is more valuable than a hundred intelligent people. A good heart is very essential. With a good heart, one can change the world. It is important to realize that man grows from the heart. When the heart is kept pure and sacred, man becomes human. You might have keen insight in regard to your sense organs, you might have a very well-developed mind, and you might be a very intelligent person, but the most important ingredient in a man's life is spiritual development. Without spiritual development, physical, mental, and intellectual development is not of much use. Life becomes purely mechanical.

We should aspire to transform our lives, to make them spiritual and not mechanical. The Sai Organizations are formed only to prove that these supreme paths are our goals.

Serve the society according to your capabilities. Do not try to show off. Do not be corrupted by egoism. Transform yourself into a divine servant. Without serving the master, you cannot become the master. Without utilizing your human qualities, you cannot become God. The members of the Sai Organization are its backbone. Embodiments of Love, the organizers among you should follow the correct path. Follow good conduct. If you choose to follow the wrong path, everyone behind you will tread the same wrong path. If leaders want to shape the universe, they should develop noble thoughts, sacred ideals, and selfless desires.

Never entertain selfish thoughts and perform self-beneficial acts in the name of service. It has become a fashion now to serve. Do not let pride and self-boasting creep in. The world today is full of materialistic possessions, and these possessions are frequently exhibited. This display of ego is the reason for changes in the world today. The destructive effects of pompous pride and ego make selfless service an essential goal for the progress of humanity.

Therefore, members of the Sai Organization should be simple, selfless, and nonegoistic. They should cultivate sacred love, the divine spirit of sacrifice, patience, and compassion. These are the qualities of the truly service-oriented members and officers.

Do not exercise your supremacy, power, and authority over others. Acknowledge everyone as being equal in power and authority. But try to maintain the harmony wherever you are, by finding the causes behind difficulties and correcting them with love. Love cannot be bound by authority. We should exercise discipline with love, not with military force. You should speak lovingly, correct others' mistakes only with love. Develop the attitude of love in everything.

Start the day with love; Fill the day with love; Spend the day with love; End the day with love; This is the way to God.

By all means, live with love. Love is God. God is omnipresent. You are all embodiments of Love. Live with love, serve with love, enjoy with love, immerse yourself in this love. This is the main aim of service. This is the primary responsibility of service. Sai Organizations should live in love. Exchange hearts with love, give love and take love, and flourish in love. But money and power have no place in our Organizations.

I do not need temples or churches. I do not need rituals

like yagnas and yagas (ritualistic worship). Our actions are yagnas (offerings), and service makes up our rituals. Hence, our Organization should not indulge in activities of collecting money for temples or rituals. I have been repeatedly saying, over and over again, that we should have no interest in or relationship with money. We are associated only with good conduct and character. However, in our Organizations, a few are still engaged in such activities. There are still those who are collecting money on the pretext that Swami came into their vision, indicating to them that they need money to build temples. This is the height of misperception.

I have never told anyone, or appeared in any vision or dream and asked them to do any such thing. They are misusing the name of the Sai Organization for collecting money from innocent people, bringing disgrace to the Organization, and making it a business arena. True, this is a business. But what kind of business? We are only in the business of exchanging love.

No one should give or take money in the name of Sai. Our membership is not made up only of poor people. We have rich people too. If any service activity is to be undertaken, and money is needed, why can't the affluent members come forward and help? These rich people should not wait to be asked. Don't they have enough? If you indulge in begging money from anyone, you will be bringing disgrace to the Sai Organization.

Make sure that the reputation of the Sai Organization is not spoiled. Other than this concern, I have no expectations from, or relationship with, the Organization.

Everyone is a member here. All are devotees. There is no distinction between members and office bearers. This Organization has been formed only for you. Every man has a right to be in it. Every man has a right to improve his humanity. Improve human values but not money values. If any group in the Organization is collecting money in the name of building a temple or performing puja (worship), such a group is not part of the Sai Organization at all. Many are attempting to carry on such business dealings.

There is nothing wrong if some of the rich people among you, within the Organization, join together to do such things. Just do not attempt to collect money by begging from door to door. Sai only wants the welfare of the universal Organization. Everybody should be happy. Everyone should improve his humanity, help his neighbor, and develop tolerance. Join hands among yourselves and come forward to serve.

There are two main points for our Organization to observe: First, do not become involved with money, government, or power. Second, do only what you can within your own limits. Let the government take care of whatever it wants to take care of. Do not use its name to enter into any activities. Do only those things which you can do with your own resources and which are within your own capabilities. When you follow these principles, even government will be helping you in your endeavors. However, do not establish any connection between the government and the Sai Organization, in relation to service.

Let us say that you initiate an activity depending on a government official's support. Later, if another official comes and does not promote your project, what will happen to your goals? Therefore, you should depend only upon yourself, not on others. That is self-confidence. One who believes in the strength of the Atma does not need any other help. Through your service to others you can reform yourself and the world. Only then can you justify your existence in a human body.

Do not try to achieve name, fame, and popularity. Try to achieve love. This is the unique goal of the Sai Organization.

Prasanthi Nilayam November 21, 1988 Sai Newsletter, Fall

SPORTSDAY MIRACLE

The months and days pass ever so quickly at Prasanthi, because we are kept busy. After Christmas, we accompanied our friends into Bangalore. It was time for their journey home. We gathered a few supplies and returned to spend the New Year with Our Lord.

This year the Annual Sports Day started on January 11th and awards were given on the 14th. The Lord during Sports Day miraculously saved a students life. I witnessed the following: One of the closing events was a spectacular jeep ride by a girl from Swami's Anantapur College. In the stadium field was a high ramp to drive up and at the end of the ramp was a large frame holding a paper banner. The girl was to drive the jeep up the ramp and fly through the paper banner, being suspended in the air for some moments then land the vehicle in an upright position and drive off.

243

The girl circled the field, driving around for what seemed like three minutes. Then suddenly the large stand holding the paper banner fell over. The banner was torn and the frame twisted. This banner stand was not fragile; it was sturdy. It startled the crowd. How could it be moved without a whisper of **wind?** There was a strangeness in the air! The field workers hastened to clear the banner stand as the girl was still driving around the field.

When it was cleared her act was again announced over the loud speaker. I was feeling a little anxious and tense. As the girl got into position, gathered speed and went up the ramp, the right rear wheel of the jeep went off the ramp. The left front wheel was also off the ramp and it appeared as if she was driving in mid-air! (see photo) What was keeping the jeep from flipping over? It continued to climb the ramp until it drove off the end, and landed upright. The girl drove away. I started breathing again.

If the banner stand had been there; the jeep wheels that were off the ramp would have gotten tangled. We heard that Swami remarked, *"The girl became frightened, lost her concentration and I saved her life."*

Miracles like this are commonplace at Prasanthi but they are still astonishing to this soul. I ask you, who but God could prop up half a jeep that is driving in mid-air? Amazing!

The following year there were several minor injuries during the Sports Day Events and at the closing ceremony Swami told the students that they should not take unnecessary risks.

"I know that you are trying to prove your courage to Swami. Anything that causes anxiety in the audience is not good."

Pongal Day Celebration followed Sports Day, then Swami left for Bombay. Robert and I stayed at Prasanthi. He did some work at the University and I started house cleaning, as I had promised to do. I sifted through all the goods I had collected from last year and gave them to the needy.

When Swami left Bombay, He returned to Brindavan so we went there. This 12th trip to visit our Lord was the best trip we ever had. He literally spoiled us. We had the best darshans ever.

Michele, my friend who lives at Prasanthi, came to see Baba in Brindavan, and shared our taxi from Bangalore to Brindavan. The night before she had been invited into Swami's house in Brindavan. That morning as we traveled together, she shared with us her glorious story of darshan in Baba's house.

She told us, "Every evening after darshan, Swami allows students and teachers to come into His home. And sometimes He invites guests. Swami sits in a large carved wooden Jula in the outer room that circles the inner room. All the men and students sit in this room. When the ladies are invited to come in they walk over the bridge through the interview room into the inner room that is also a circle. The ladies cannot see Baba very well except through the door-way. His face is blocked by the students, the door frame and the big pillar on the Jula. In

245

order to see Him you must sit on the extreme left."

She continued, "But my joy was the pleasure of again sitting in His house, remembering, smelling the fragrance, feeling His footsteps on the floor, and hearing His sweet voice." She told us, "Swami spontaneously picks students or guests to give talks and Baba sometimes gives a Discourse. They also sing a few bhajans. Afterwards, He walks past all the ladies giving darshan and then distributes Prasad. It is a very special time with Baba."

That evening after darshan, Swami gave Bhajans in the Wedding Hall. It was the first time I had sat this close to Swami during Bhajans since 1979 in Ooty. I lingered and was one of the last to leave. It was Thursday February 6.

When I came out a devotee told me that my husband went inside Swami's house and came out looking for me. So I started walking through the gates with a Seva Dal close behind me. She asked Mataji if I had permission and Mataji said, YES! I wanted to hug her but it was not appropriate.

I still could hear my friends words from that morning. Was Swami having her preparing me for tonight? When she spoke of her experience today, I would never have believe that it was a glimpse of Robert's and my future. Swami was full of surprises on this trip.

I found myself following in her footsteps: walking over the bridge through the interview room, into the inner room. Since she had prepared me, I knew exactly where to sit.... and I could see Swami! It was happening too fast, I couldn't believe it was happening. How did I get there? How did Robert get there? Oh Lord, I too must soak in the fragrance, feel the floor, observe the room and people, keep my eyes on you and enjoy this unforgettable moment. It was too good to be true!

During Swami's discourse, I heard 'Cuckoo! Cuckoo! Cuckoo!' As I looked around the room I noticed that Swami had a cuckoo clock and when the cuckoo stopped, the little dancers came out and danced around to a tune. A Cuckoo Clock in God's House. I chuckled. Two mystical hours of sitting in Swami's house was coming to an end. I listened to Him sing a Bhajan, then He gave us darshan and prasad for the Seva Dals to pass out.

Robert and I were so grateful to Swami for allowing us to come into His house. This blessing continued every night while Swami was in Brindavan.

While we were there our son wrote us that he, his sweet wife Patricia, and their first child, Christian, now one year old were coming to see Swami in April, at Kodaikanal. This was extremely good news. We had missed their wedding but Swami was blessing us to be here with their first born. We decided to rent a house in Kodai because it would be better to prepare our own food especially since they were bringing Christian. The cost of hotels in Kodai is high and if we could rent a home with two or three bedrooms we could share the expense and the cost would be less.

We wrote a note asking Swami if we should go to Kodai before April and rent a house for the month. Swami came over and took the note from Robert. I was a little surprised that He was allowing us to do this because it is a long trip but I also knew that accommodation in Kodai in April is very difficult to find because it is the high season in the mountains during the hot summer.

Swami went back to Prasanthi and we stayed with Him till Shivarathri. Swami had all night bhajans, two discourses, and fed us a meal afterwards. The energy level after these festivals is high. Baba just pours out His love and the devotees pour out theirs. When I'm in this state, I just like to sit and enjoy the inner bliss, but there had been very few opportunities for this. We were leaving for Kodaikanal. It was March 3, and we decided this would be the best time. We really couldn't wait much longer if we wanted to rent a house.

We took a plane to Coimbatore, where we were met by Vijay and Vanita, best friends of my son Craig. They were the best man and maid of honor at Craig and Pat's wedding. Now they were living in Coimbatore and had two sweet daughters. They cared for us as if we were their own family. Their love and kindness made us feel Swami's Presence.

They made absolutely sure that we had a good driver for the four hour trip up the mountains and he would stay with us while we looked around. It was hot on the plains but as we traveled up the mountains it began to cool off. It was very refreshing. March, April and May in India are sweltering hot except in hill country.

You know Sai Baba is ever present with each of us; and He tells us this over and over. It is not always so obvious when we are at home doing the normal routine things, because our ego is familiar and thinks it is in control. But as soon as we step out on a limb, remove ourself from the norm, we can see His Divine Hand is clearly present.

A real estate agent is not a term that is understood in Kodai. So we drove around looking for a sign. We found a Construction Office that had the world real-estate symbol in the corner of their sign. Robert knocked on the door. No one was in the office but he could see a picture of Sai Baba standing next to a man on the desk. It reminded me of the old western movies. We were on the India Trail looking for signs! Thanks to Swami; He certainly made the sign clear enough.

We returned later and discovered the man in the photo with Baba was also incharge of some construction work being done on Sai Baba's home. He took us to see two homes. The first house was very nice and had a spectacular view because it was on the side of a mountain. It made me feel like I was out on a cat-walk overlooking the Grand Canyon. I really enjoyed the view.

The second house was also first class. The shades were drawn as we looked around and not until we returned to the first floor did I notice the four foot Ganesh sitting in an alcove in the Dining Room. There was also an altar on the opposite wall with a picture of Shirdi Sai. Since my son Craig was devoted to Ganesh, a four foot Ganesh even we didn't miss! Sai was leaving a clear trail.

It was a lovely house with three bedrooms and two baths, large living room and dining room. The kitchen I was told had the "only refrigerator" in Kodai. It would be so handy for the baby's milk. The yard was lovely, some flowers blooming even though the mountains had a severe drought and water shortage. We were assured that they had plenty of water. The only drawback we could foresee was the dirt road to the house rutted with big holes, on an incline and not too wide. But the house was luxury for India and superseded our requirements. Thank you Swami.

When we returned to Vijay and Vanita's home, we called Craig and Patricia and relayed to them the gift from Ganesh and Swami. Their tickets were confirmed and in a month they would be here. It seemed to good to be true. We would all be together with Swami in Kodaikanal. What a lovely re-union.

We finalized our plans. Vijay and Vanita were going to bring Craig and Patricia to Kodaikanal.

When we arrived in Bangalore, Swami had left Prasanthi for the summer and was staying in Brindavan. Since we had not packed up the apartment; we returned to Prasanthi. Then we said our good-bye to some dear friends who stay on there even though the heat is unbearable. I have only praise for their devotion to Sai Baba.

I was tired from the heat, cleaning, packing and traveling. In the taxi, I rested my head back on the seat, after I could no longer see Prasanthi. I always feel a little heavy hearted when I leave God's house. Our trip had been glorious, thus far. We had had satsang with the most wonderful people, plus all the extra Grace from Swami. I had always wanted a family interview and I wondered if this would come true. I imagined Swami talking with our children and playing with the baby. But

I was drifting too far off in the future. All I could do was to put the wish in my Sai Treasure Chest of hopes and dreams... to which only He has the key.

At Brindavan every morning Robert went into Swami's garden with the boys and had darshan. One morning Robert asked Swami, "Can we have permission to travel with you to Kodaikanal and Ooty?" Sai leaned towards Robert and took out the Sarva Dharma medal hidden inside his shirt, looked at it, then placed it back inside. As He was doing this Sai replied, *"Yes, Yes, Yes."* Robert then repeated the request to Baba, as if to confirm what he asked.

In the evening, the men always went into Swami's house. Each night when the ladies lined up, we never knew if Swami would send word for us to come in or not. There were maybe 3 nights that we did not come in during this two week period. I'm sure the Lord was getting bombarded with our inward pleas.

When we got the signal, Mataji would give her OK. and there was a hustle and bustle to get into the room and find a good seat. Sometimes when we came in Swami would be standing in the doorway talking to the boys. He loved to tease and play with them. Always their eyes were reverently focused on Swami. The feel of the marble was cool on my feet as I moved across the floor, quickly glancing for a spot. I can't believe how fast these older ladies that come in here move! Sometimes I felt like I was sliding into home plate. Put down the cushion and sit. It was always crowded on the side where you could see Baba. Even then if His swing, the Jula, was too far back there was no view. It was like playing hide and seek with the Lord. But when Swami gave a Discourse, He stood up and then more devotees could see Him. There was always the choice of sitting by the wall tightly jammed to see Baba, or to sit on the other side, in the front row where Swami walked by, as He left the room. Then He would call four boys and five or six would come. He would give them Prasad to pass out to the students and men. Then they would place a box or two in the ladies room. Then Swami would walk up stairs and all our necks would stretch to get the last look for the night.

Robert told me that when the ladies take Prasad and leave the room, all the students and men come into this inner room. The inner circle room is open all the way to the second floor ceiling. There is a balcony that circles the second floor and the upstairs rooms are entered from the balcony. It is impossible to see Swami when He is walking around the balcony unless He leans forward. He then waves good-night to the boys. And on several occasions, Swami played with them popping up in different places. How the boys love it! The big boys too!

There was a problem hearing the men or students speaking from the ladies room. Robert would always share with me the highlights that he could remember. One night I asked Robert. "Does Swami ever ask the ladies to speak?" "No," said Robert. The very next night Swami asked a woman guest to speak. I heard the voice inside say, "What does he know?" There goes another ego-chop for Robert.

The woman sat in front, in the honored guest place.

This time we could hear. Swami was so friendly to her. She was at one time the Vice-Chancellor of Mysore University who had taken another position in Delhi after speaking with Swami. Sai Baba was her life. One thing she said that shows the humor and closeness of her relationship with Swami, I want to share with you. She said, "There was a period in my life when Swami at darshan only gave me His back. I never saw His front. "But, Oh Swami...'**back darshan** is as beautiful as your front!" Did Baba laugh and we all roared because we certainly were familiar with that experience.

The next evening, I was sitting way in the back. I heard Swami speaking and my husband, Robert answering.

Swami, *"America, when are you going back?"*

Robert, "In May, Swami."

Swami, *"May."*

Swami, *"Are you going to Kodaikanal?"*

Robert, "Yes Swami."

Swami, *"Where's wife?"*

Robert, (pointing in the ladies room) "Around the corner."

Swami, *"How do you know?"* (laughter)

Swami, *"What are you doing in America?"*

Robert, "I'm retired, staying with you Swami."

Swami, *"huh?"*

Robert, "I'm retired now."

Students repeat, "He's retired."

Robert, "I'm staying in India, Swami."

Swami, *"Are you doing Sai's work? In the Sai Organization?"*

Robert, "Yes, Swami."

Swami, *"What is your wife doing?"*

Swami answers the question.

Swami said, *"writing, writing, writing. She is a good lady. You're, eh not."* (laughter)

Swami, *"Whats the name of that book?"*

Robert, "Vision of Sai."

Swami, *"What's the meaning of the book? book!"*

Robert, "Yes, Swami. It's about you guiding us all these years."

Swami, *What's the name of this book?*

Robert, "Vision of Sai."

Swami, *"Vision of Sai."*

Swami looks into the ladies room and calls loudly. *"Where is your husband?"*

Since there were only two ladies in the room from America with husbands in the next room, the ladies in front who could hear Swami thought He was talking to Barbara Sinclair who was also in front. Finally, I got the word from Mrs. Hedgemahdi that Swami is calling me. I knelt up.

Meanwhile Swami is continuing to talk with Robert.

Swami, *"What is her name?"*

Robert, "Rita."

Swami, *"Second name."*

Robert, "Bruce."

Swami, *"Rita Bruce, yes I know."*

Swami again looks in the ladies room and calls out putting His hand to His mouth, *"Where is your husband?"*

(I'm thinking to myself, there's that same question, I've heard twice before and gave wrong answers....)

Rita, "Only you know, Swami."

Swami turns to speak again with Robert.

Swami, *"Where are you staying in Kodaikanal?"*

Robert, "We have a house we found."

Swami, *"Where?"*

Robert, "Near Zion School. Very expensive, Swami"

Swami, *"Very expensive. Some hotels charging 3000 rupies, night, no food. Don't waste money; misuse of money is evil.*

Afterwards, on the way back to our hotel Robert talked; I listened. As I could not hear the dialogue with Swami from the ladies' side, he shared what he could remember. My mind replayed the questions that Swami asked on Kodaikanal. I said, "Robert, we thought that Swami sent us to Kodaikanal to find a house for our family's use. But, now I don't believe that was the reason. I think Swami wants to use the house. It's not our house; it's Swami's house. While we were in Kodai, our real-estate agent told us that Sai Baba has very little room at His Kodaikanal house for guests because of the students and teachers. I think Swami may want to use this house for one of His guests. Anyway tomorrow, how about giving Swami a note? Thanking Him for the house and telling Him that the house is His and we would be happy if He sent us someone to share it."

The next morning Robert gave the note to Swami. After darshan, I received a wonderful gift. One of the students had taped the dialogue between Robert and Swami and gave it to me as a keepsake. I was thrilled. Swami thinks of everything. Tears came to my eyes because of the thoughtfulness and sensitivity of our Lord Sai. Such a little insignificant thing, no need for His concern, and yet how His special touches of Selfless Love affected and changed the fiber of my Heart. His Love is so overwhelming, no mother nor father on earth could ever fill the need that each of us as children deserve and want. No wonder there is such a craving deep in our souls that hunger for this Selfless Love that only God can give. He was filling the cavity in my Heart. Who else but God would do so much?

Several days later, I was ill and did not go for darshan. It was a big decision, but my health needed attention. When Robert came home He was excited about the evening's events. I could hardly wait to hear.

Swami got a new car that night.... a maroon jaguar!

After the talks and bhajans, Swami went outside, and gave darshan and the boys sang. Swami then broke coconuts and blessed the car and the coconut water flew all over Robert. Swami smiled and Robert got padnamaskar.

Swami got into the car and drove around the compound. When He was in sight again, Swami's head was sticking out of the top of the car giving "Sun Visor Roof Darshan." His sense of humor is delightful! Yes, the car had a sun roof and Little Swami was standing on the front seat with His Black Halo blowing in the wind from the car roof. Everyone loved it!

Swami's sense of humor is something I would like to share with you. Robert has been exposed to it profusely these last three years. My, does the Lord love to tease and play with us. One man asked Swami, "Can I merge with you, Swami?" Baba replied, *"But you're so fat; and I'm so small, how can you merge with Swami?"*

One day when Robert was in Baba's house with the students in Brindavan, Swami was in another room and called *"America."* He came to the door to get Robert. Swami had a man there and they were looking at a table with attached chairs.

Swami said to Robert, *"Sit down. What do you think?"*

Robert wiggled around a little and said, "Swami, too small for westerners."

Swami replied, *"I think so too!"*

The man standing there said, "I'll make the seats 2 inches larger."

257

"Yes," replied Swami, *"Westerners, you know, Suprabottoms!"*

It was a great play on the Sanskrit word Suprabhatham.

They were the tables and chairs for the new canteen in Prasanthi.

Several nights later we had another surprise! Before all the ladies were seated, Swami asked Robert, *"America, do you speak English?"*

Robert replied, "Midwestern English." (we live in the midwest.) Swami was referring to the King's English.

Swami continued, *"I want you to talk."*

Robert stood up.

"Not now, sit down, later," said Baba.

Swami was giving Robert an opportunity quickly to prepare. I was astonished when I heard Robert's voice from the other room. He spoke loud and we ladies could hear. He spoke on self-confidence and the rare privilege it was for all of us to be here with Baba. He talked about the role of Swami as our Mother, Father, Teacher and Friend. When Robert spoke on the role of the Father, he looked at Swami and told the boys "in this role He shakes His ego finger at us scolding us." And Robert shook his ego finger as an example. Swami nodded His head, in agreement.

Robert spoke from his heart and I could feel Swami's Love. I was so happy for him. It was so crowded that

Robert had a hard time getting close enough to Swami to kiss His foot. The guest speakers get to kiss Baba's feet before and after their talks. Swami picked His foot up and Robert held the tiny brown foot in his hand as he took padnamaskar. That night after the ladies had left the building and Swami came to the balcony to say goodnight to the boys, He looked at Robert and shook His finger at the boys!

That evening as I was walking to our taxi, Barbara Sinclair said, "You'll get an interview tomorrow. Baba has given each of His guest speakers an interview after their talk." I told Robert what she said and we both had high hopes!

The next morning I got specific instructions from Robert. He said, "Now after darshan, if Swami doesn't call you; He may call me. So sit where you can watch the gate after Swami goes in and if He calls me for an interview, I can find you."

We were prepared. I was not called at darshan, so I shifted my seat to watch the gate.

Inside the garden, Swami walked over to the interview bridge and called Robert. He quickly went to Swami and asked, "Interview Swami, should I get wife?" Baba smiled, slapped him on the shoulders several times and said, *"No, no, no."*

Meanwhile I was still obeying orders and watching the gate. A man came running out waving. I looked, no it was not Robert. The lady sitting right next to me got up. (she must have had orders too!) They got the interview. Isn't

He a tease! But isn't it also proof of His Omnipresence. The lady was sitting right next to me!

The next morning before darshan, Sai Baba told me inside: "Hold open your hands and spread your fingers as far a part as possible. I will fill your hands till they overflow with my Grace. You and Robert will be my guests and attend the special sessions in my house in Kodai." I prayed to Swami that if this message was correct would He please give me Padnamaskar during darshan. Swami Dear, did give me Padnamaskar.

After darshan a girl came to me with a rose that she offered to Swami. She said that she wanted me to have it. I never saw the girl before. But I joyfully accepted the rose. Do I dare dream for more?

When Robert and I met after darshan; we shared stories. Inside the garden Swami had played a little game with Jim Sinclair and Robert. They were both standing together. Swami reached down and picked up a handful of candy from a student's tray and threw it to the boys. Then He took another handful and threw it. The third handful He pretended to throw to Jim and Robert. They started to catch it and moved forward. Swami again threw, in pretense. Their reflexes again responded. The third time He called them over. With a closed fist, Swami put candy in Jim's hand and did the same to Robert. Swami said, *"Team."*

After Swami left they each opened their hand. Jim had three pieces and Robert had five pieces. The exact number for Jim's family who were now present, since one of his daughters had just left, and one remained. And five for our family which included Craig, Patricia, and Christian. The word "team," we're not sure what Swami meant. They are both fathers, both Americans, and both went to Kodaikanal.

Considering Swami's inner message to me about filling my hands with His Grace and then Sai actually filling Roberts hand with sweets made me feel more certain that the message was correct.

One evening, Swami gave a Discourse in the Marriage Hall after Bhajans. Anytime Swami speaks it is a joy to be in His Presence, especially at Brindavan, as it is smaller and more intimate than at Prasanthi.

That evening, Swami called the Principal of Brindavan College, Anil Kumar to do the interpreting into English. There was an electricity between them that I had never seen before. Principal Kumar has a relaxed, personal relationship with Baba. It came across throughout the entire discourse, sometimes in their humor, gesture or laughter. The mood was lighthearted.

I had heard from devotees the following statement, and now Baba had confirmed for me that it is true.

"When you touch the Lord's Feet His Divinity enters into you. This Divine fire burns defects and all the sins. Being dear to the Lord is not enough; you must be near. Near and dear; love and proximity must be together because every touch of God makes you free from Karma." Discourse Brindavan March 1992

As March came to an end, so did school at Brindavan. The last day of school, Swami blessed each student with Padnamaskar and gave them packets of Vibhuthi. The presence of Sai Mother stood before us that evening speaking with so much love and compassion to the students. The boys were pleading for Swami not to leave, as they reached out to touch Him. The Lord seemed to linger in response to their feelings.

For some students, those who were graduating, this could be their last darshan as a student in Swami's house. I remembered speaking with an alumni student some years ago who told me that the joy of being really close to Swami's form is equally painful when the students must leave. No one wanted to leave the Love of Mother Sai. You could feel their pangs of sadness and sorrow.

KODAIKANAL

The ashram was experiencing "Kodai Fever". Devotees were packing, making reservations and travel arrangements. Swami's guests were arriving, one couple whom we knew, Dr. Jack Hislop and Victoria. Swami had invited them to join Him in Kodaikanal this year. Robert told Jack about us renting a house in Kodai and they were welcome to stay with us.

Each year, during Summer holidays Swami selects some students to accompany Him. Puttaparthi is very hot in April and the mountains are a glorious retreat from the heat. These Kodai students were the center of Sai's attention. They would be His guests and stay inside His house. Can you imagine, 30 days of living close to His Divine Form? What an incentive, a challenge to work towards during the school years. It must be the "Grand Prize" for any student in Baba's College.

263

The selection of the boys from Prasanthi and Brindavan was finally made. Swami selected 28 students and had them all assembled on the Brindavan campus preparing for the Ultimate Experience in their young lives.

The act of selecting students - good companions - reminds me of Swami's words to us. He says, *"Tell me your company; I'll tell you what you are. You will change when you are with good people. Good company is necessary for a good son."* Kodaikanal April 1992

A day before we were to leave Sai Baba gave last minute invitations to some of the teachers. Swami keeps all of the devotees, regardless of the rank and file, strung out. Position simply makes no difference to Swami. These divisions are only in our mind.

Swami's Love is beyond human comprehension. But His example shows the depth of His Love and communicates His Message in a way that we can understand. Through Swami's example we experience the GREATEST LOVE KNOWN TO MAN", and eventually realize that we too can be a living testimony of His Divinity. This Majestic Love is an unknown in our world. And yet, this kind of Love is exactly what God feels for each and every living thing in our Universe. Quite simply, He Loves us; untouched by any ego.

Sai Baba says, *"Whether you believe it or not, I shall tell you one thing. There is not the slightest trace of self-interest in Me. Whatever I do, whatever paths I pursue, everything is intended for the happiness of all, for the good of all, and for the improvement of all. Not a single action of Mine is undertaken for the satisfaction of My own personal desires. Desire is something alien to Me. All My wishes are only to promote the welfare of the world. That all the world may be happy is the only objective of Sai."* Sathya Sai Speaks, Vol. XI, p. 59

In the remaining days before departure, Swami called the boys into an interview to inform them about the trip. He told them what they would need and gave them the responsibility to prepare.

He said in a discourse one evening in Kodai: *"The atmosphere in Prasanthi is different than here. It's very hot, thin dress. In Kodai its cool, you must wear a sweater. It is your mistake if you are not prepared. It is the same with the outside world. It is bad; and you must prepare yourself."*

You could see the "Kodai Fever" gathering momentum as the days peeled away and the time to leave was coming near.

Jack and Victoria Hislop accepted Robert's invitation to stay with us. We wanted to care for them as Baba would. They were His guests' not ours. Since they were traveling by plane to Coimbatore, we again called upon our friends Vijay and Vanita Kumar to assist them.

The Hislops would be their guests, in Swami's name and they would make sure they had the same driver that we used because he knew the exact location of the house we rented. Directions were very difficult to give because these dirt roads had no street signs. No one could have found that house except the same driver. Swami's goodness just takes care of every detail.

The day before we left, Swami gave each of the students going to Kodai a camera and materialized a pill for them to take before they left. It seemed that last year, some of the students got bus sick traveling around the mountain curves. Swami was using prevention.

We, too, packed and were told what time to be at the ashram to join Swami's caravan. We got there early around 4 a.m. and much to my surprise there must have been at least 20 to 30 cars lined-up in the street. I thought, "My! How Swami's Mission has spread; years ago when He went to Ooty, there were only four cars." The nostalgia of yester-year crept into my heart.

We went into the back garden, received Sai Baba's darshan, the coconuts were broken and Swami left. Our driver went a different way saying he was taking a short cut. We drove for about 45 minutes and then the driver called out, "Here comes Swami." I turned to look behind our car, I saw nothing. Then as I turned my head to the front, zoom.... went Swami's car past us on the other side of the road, with a long parade of cars behind him. We weren't following Swami; we were going in the opposite direction! I guess there are **NO** shortcuts to Sai Baba.

I inquired, "Why are we going in the opposite direction?" Apparently, he had to secure a permit to cross the border. Instead of getting the pass the day before, our driver waited. So we were held up in a queue with the other cars that had no pass. We were told by the driver that it is very dangerous to follow Swami because all the devotees want to be behind Swami's car. The drivers are recklessly passing each other and they take unnecessary risks.

Our driver reported that two cars already had accidents. We told the driver, not to worry about catching up with Swami. Just drive normally.

It was so hot, as we were driving across the plains and desert. The driver felt very hot so Robert would wet a handkerchief and place it on his head. He did the same for me. The air would evaporate the water and give a cooling sensation. The higher the sun rose in the sky; the worse it got. I could hardly wait till we reached the mountains. It would be 6 or 7 hours before this happened. It was over 110 degree's. I was so glad the Hislops were flying to Coimbatore.

Even the cars were having trouble. We stopped many times checking on other drivers whose taxis were overheated. We too, had to stop for water and to cool the engine. The day's journey was dragging longer and longer. We were well stocked with water and oranges. This was not the time to become dehydrated.

During the journey, Swami had joined the students on the bus instead of traveling in the comfort of His air-conditioned car. Because of the intense heat, one of the students in the bus took a piece of cardboard to fan Our Lord Sai. Baba refused the fan and told them, *"I suffer what you suffer."*

Over and over, Sai Baba shows us His compassion and all serving Love. He not only gives to mankind but He gives in an egoless and effortless way. In all the time that I have had the privilege of being with Sai Baba, I have

never seen Him give any sign of ego.

He never speaks about Himself. He does not ask for physical comforts. He is always in complete control of Himself. And above all, He is **always available** to us regardless of what month or what year it is.

His Divine Mission is fifty years old. He has been giving darshan, day in and day out. Translated into our terms, "on the job" seven days a week, twelve months a year, for fifty years. It is inconceivable that a human would work continuously for others, not collecting any pay for himself. Even during His summer vacation to Ooty or Kodaikanal, thousands of visitors sit in His yard waiting for His Blessings and Darshan. His vacations merely mean change of address; not work schedule.

As we traveled up the mountain with the laggers; all passed by the "fast track" cars earlier in the day, I welcomed the slower pace. The higher we climbed the cooler the air. I was tired. We had been in the car since 4 a.m. and it was now close to six p.m. The journey took much longer than we were told.

As we drove over the bumpy road to the house, we prayed that the real estate man acted as per our agreement to have the house cleaned and the key left with the staff that lived behind the house... the caretaker and his family. We had written him a letter telling him when we would arrive.

It seemed that the real estate man had left town and the family did not have the key, nor were they able to get in and clean. So I sat on the steps and called on my "God

Mother Sai" for help. Since they spoke very little English, and we were ignorant of their native tongue, communication was a problem. It took awhile to decipher each other's words and gestures.

Our taxi driver helped. The caretaker's son, then went with the taxi to try and find a key. We sat in silence, on the porch step watching the sun go down behind the mountain range, and the village people as they walked by. This house was also perched on the side of a mountain, and we could see the homes and huts that dotted the slopes.

The key arrived and Mary, the wife of the caretaker, welcomed us into the home. It was wonderful to be there. She spoke a little English; the rest of her family did not. Mary was the sweetest woman and she captured all of our hearts!

The next morning we went to darshan, at Swami's house in Kodai. His house is 100 yards from the road up a steep drive-way. The darshan lines queued up across the street in a large park area that surrounded the lake. It was a beautiful setting. The mountains, lake, pine trees, flowers and cool air all adorn the Blessed visit of Sai.

At the top of the driveway was Baba's front yard that he used for darshan. The men sat on the far left side of Sai's house and the ladies to the right. Swami concerned with His devotees, had shelters made for darshan this year. He had had cement slabs poured and covered them with a roof for the devotees because April was the monsoon season and it would rain on many afternoons.

When the afternoon rains came this year, and the number of visitors expanded outside the shelter, many got wet. So Our Dear considerate Lord, canceled darshan the next afternoon. Some of the devotees sent Sai Baba a telegram. "We don't care if we get wet or cold. All we want is Your darshan. Love. Your Devotees."

The following day there was an announcement made. "Afternoon darshan would resume." Their love and prayers softened the Lord's heart.

Sai said, *"In the Dwapara age, Indra caused a heavy downpour. The people, who were affected by the deluge, prayed to the Lord: "Oh Lord! We and our cattle are suffering from this downpour. Save us from the rain." The Lord replied "I cannot stop this rain. Whatever has to happen in Nature has to go on. But I have the right to protect you from its adverse effects. Rain comes according to the laws of Nature. These natural phenomena should go on in their respective ways. But, having regard to your devotion and prayers, I shall lift this hill and provide shelter to all of you. But I will not stop the rain." (The reference is to the lifting of the Govardhana mountain by Sri Krishna).*

"Now the wind has the power to blow out a lamp. The Divine has endowed the lamp with the power to shed light. The powers of the wind and of light are derived from God. But it is foolish for anyone to order the wind not to blow out the lamp. What one can do is to protect the lamp from the blast of wind by fixing a chimney. This is within human capacity.

"Through these examples you should learn how to regulate the forces of Nature and not seek to go against

270

natural laws. It follows that man has the freedom to enjoy the things provided by the Creator. But man should exercise his discrimination to determine what are beneficial for him and what are not fit to be used." Sanathana Sarathi, July 1992 p. 162

Dr. Hislop talked about the power of prayer and told the following story. "One year, Swami sent me to Brindavan to tell the students that He would not come as planned. His trip would be delayed. After delivering the message, I went back to Prasanthi, and found that Swami was leaving as He originally planned. I asked Swami, "Why, Swami did you send me to Brindavan to tell the boys you would be delayed? And now I find that you are going to Brindavan as originally planned." Baba said, *"Because they are praying for Swami to come."*

Another building had been constructed near Swami's house. This building had two floors. On the first floor was a large beautiful Bhajan Hall. Swami also gave interviews in an adjacent room.

The drive-way turned left past the New Bhajan Hall, and ended at Sai's house. Everything was immaculate and beautiful. Trees and flowers graced the drive-way, yard and home. No wonder Swami enjoyed spending His summer holiday here, with the boys. It was paradise.

This environment was much different from Ooty. Baba's house was newer, not a school setting like Ooty but a home that was in a residential neighborhood. "Imagine being a neighbor of Baba's!" Some neighbors sat on their front porch and got darshan.

We had a beautiful morning darshan, Swami came out of the house onto His porch then walked across the drive-way to look over the side, giving darshan to the devotees below. There was Sai Baba's magnificent face leaning over this balcony with flowers from the garden framing His face. It was the sweetest picture and a photographer's heaven.

Robert said, "We have received permission to come into Swami's house after evening darshan." The ladies were to line-up in the driveway leading to the house. I felt as if I were dreaming. All I could say was, "Thank You, Thank You, Thank You, Swami."

The Hislops would be here tomorrow and our children four days later, I had a day's house cleaning ahead of me. I wanted everything in readiness for them. Mary and I worked side by side. Cleaning, scrubbing, washing all the kitchen dishes and utensils with hot water. I didn't want anyone to get sick. We had heard that many devotees got sick in Kodai last year.

We washed the shelves and drawers, lined them with clean paper, everything including mattresses and pillows went outside to beat and air in the sunlight. Baba tells us, *"Whatever you do; do wholeheartedly. Not artificially!"* Kodaikanal April 1992

Afterwards, I picked some flowers from the yard and placed them on the altar, thanking Ganesh and Shirdi Sai as well. I thought it was quite interesting that these two deities were in the house. Mrs. Hislop is very devoted to Shirdi Sai, and Craig is to Ganesh.... both being guests who would be staying here. Swami attends to the most

272

minute details.

I hurriedly prepared for afternoon darshan. I had been thinking of going into Swami's house all day. Robert and I could hardly wait. I was beginning to feel like the Kodai students, joyful beyond belief.

I followed the other ladies and lined up. I guessed there were about twenty of us that first evening. The Seva - Dals had a tremendous job trying to separate who was a guest and who was not. It would take days before a working pattern would emerge for the Seva - Dals. There were twice the number of devotees this year compared to last year. Everywhere you go with Baba, the crowds are swelling. How much time do we have before His prophesy, *"There will be so many people that I will appear as a small dot of orange in the distance,"* comes true?

We walked single file up a few stairs to the porch. Then through the doorway into the living room. This was where the students and men were seated all around Baba's chair. The ladies were seated in the dining room, right behind the living room. We were separated by a wooden banister. The dining room was one step higher than the living room so that improved our view of Swami. This time we peeked through the spokes of the banister.

His home was lovely. Not as big as Brindavan, it was the size of a normal home. So Swami was very close to us even though we were in the dining room. The living room was small and the men were very crowded and they had to squeeze to fit everyone inside.

There was a fireplace in the corner, then Sai's table with all of His mail placed beside His chair. Above Swami's chair was another cuckoo clock! On the wall to the left of Baba's chair was a sofa. There was no other furniture in this room, all the available space was given to us.

Every night, Swami would come in through the door on the men's side. Then He slowly inched His way towards His chair. First, He walked between the men who were seated at the back, and next He went to the students who were gathered around His footstool and chair in the front of the room. During this time the men got to hold His feet or touch His hand. Sometimes Swami would pat them on the shoulder, give a smile or speak to them. This would become a familiar evening ritual. It was especially nice for the men to sit where Swami walked by.

Sai had a man and a student give a talk or sing before His nightly discourse. Sometimes the students would chant the Vedas. This pleased Baba and He acted like a proud father whose child had accomplished a great feat.

Swami wanted the students to have self-confidence and gave them every opportunity during the day to practice speaking and singing in His Divine Presence, as he guided and corrected them.

He told them, *"Make an effort to Practice. Why listen to Sai's teachings without practice. What is heard must be transferred to the Heart! Everything today goes from the head to the mouth. Everything should go from the head through the heart."*

274

Swami held His hand so sweetly on His heart as He made this statement. He told us that what we learn; we speak. Knowledge goes from the head to the mouth. But what we learn must go through the heart. How many times He has told us that Love can only be expressed by service. Since love comes from the heart, He wants us to take His teachings, by-pass the mouth, and give love from the heart in actions of service, to practice what He teaches.

He also told us, *"When you love God, you follow Him and His commands."* Kodai April 18, 1992

The devotees and students mostly spoke about their personal experiences and how Swami helped them and/or their families. Some spoke of how He intervened and saved their life. It delighted me to watch Swami respond to the speakers when they were sharing their personal experiences with Baba. It's one thing to tell a Baba story to others and another to tell a Baba story in Sai Baba's Presence! His humility touched my heart.

Sai Baba told us that His topic for the month would be "Saints Lives." Swami would teach us about the character, behavior and sacrifice of the great souls that lived on earth. He would explain to us our role and correct conduct in the Guru Disciple relationship.

"There are three types of Self-surrender. The first affirms, I am yours, the second asserts, you are mine, and the third declares, you and I are one, the same. Each is just a step in the rising series and the last is the highest step of all.

In the first stage the Lord is fully free and the devotee is fully bound. It is like the cat and kitten; the cat shifts the kitten about as it wills; the kitten just mews and accepts whatever happens. This attitude is very gentle and is within easy reach of all. The second, the devotee binds the Lord, who is to that extent unfree! The devotee can tie up the Lord with His Love by devotion that overwhelms and overpowers his egoism. When man is full of this type of devotion the Lord will Himself Bless Him with everything he needs; His grace will fulfill all his wants."

When the discourse concluded, Swami would get prasad for the students and Seva - Dals to pass out. It reminded me of my mother's house when it was time for the children to leave, she would give them a "goody bag". He gave us sumptuous treats of sweets every night as we left.

I realized that in those past two hours Swami managed to carry me away in the aura of His Divine Love. I looked around at the other ladies as we started down the driveway, and saw that I wasn't the only one His Heart had captured.

Swami told us that evening, *"Swami could change your life; and it would never change back again."*

The next morning, April 7th, this was the day that Dr. and Mrs. Hislop would arrive. After darshan, Mary went with me to shop for food supplies. We prepared menus and meal schedules. My children would arrive on the 11th and then the house would be full. Swami certainly had me in a role that I was very comfortable in.

When Jack and Victoria arrived it felt as if Swami's Love and Light had come into our house. Robert and I could ask Jack any spiritual question. He always replied with what "Swami says." It was like having Baba there to answer and clear up any spiritual misconceptions. As I was feeding them food; they were feeding us Spiritual food. God Blessed our house.

Swami says, *"You are only a bank manager giving back to God what is His with the check of sacrifice."* Kodaikanal April 19, 1992.

Our family arrived at 8:30 p.m. on Rama's Feast Day. The reunion was a happy one and Christian had grown so much in our five months absence. He was tired and in a strange, new environment and clung to mom and dad. He was so cute. What a joy it is for Robert and I being grandparents!

The following morning at darshan our children were blessed by Baba. I had a front row and Patricia sat directly behind with Christian. Children are not allowed in the front row. When Swami got close, Patricia handed the baby to me. I held the child up for Swami, He put His hand on Christian, blessing him. Swami said, *"The children have come!"* Baba smiled so sweetly at Patricia.

After darshan, Craig told us that Baba had given him vibhuthi and padnamaskar. I can only imagine the joy it gave to Craig and Patricia for them to be received with so much love. It takes great sacrifice to bring a small child to India and faith that Sai will keep him healthy and quiet during darshan. Patricia spent almost every darshan, holding, walking and caring for Christian. It was a real challenge keeping a one year old occupied and quiet. Parenting and sacrifice are synonymous.

Swami said, *"The mother sacrifices her all for rearing the child, protecting him and bringing him up well. Hence, the sweetness manifest in maternal love cannot be found in any other object or experience. What greater sweetness is there in our land than a mother's love?"* Sanathana Sarathi June 1993, p. 162

Swami was with the students twenty-four hours a day, some slept outside Baba's room. Sai Baba was an extraordinary example of the ideal role of Mother and Father. His behavior was perfect. The absolute role model for parents. If any student got sick, Swami would immediately respond. And when they ate, Swami walked among them checking to see that they had everything they needed, constantly making sure they had enough food and drink. He was thinking only of them; not of Himself.

Sai said, *"Actions should be selfless. Taken for the sake of action; not for the results of action. Action is not great unless it is offered as selfless service."* Kodaikanal April 1992

I thought about my grandchild, this innocent soul embarking on a new journey, which is his life, and it can be influenced by good or bad values. I began to compare the spiritual climate of these students with the students living in America. I again realized that our children and grandchildren are not receiving the moral messages from our world that Swami says they need. The same old ache is still in my heart, the innocence of our young being influenced by greed and corruption. The two sources of materialism.

The message of self-interest is fashionable and being reinforced in all the facets of communication, parents, people and peers. Even if we stop the behavior in our home what can we do when it is duplicated by hundreds of students in school? What chance do our children have? Even so, first we as parents have the responsibility to stop it at home. We, too are being "taken in" by the world consciousness. Baba keeps telling us that we are supporting the image of the "ME" generation. We are buying and doing everything possible to give our children pleasure, and not teaching them how to give others pleasure. They become self-centered and self-indulgent children, teen-agers and adults.

Baba said, *"Today the children have no respect for the mother. Mothers have also little concern for the children. With the result that the Kali age has become "Kalaha" age - the age of discord.*

"Who are responsible for this situation? The mothers are the root cause. It is because of the pampering of the children in all sorts of ways by the mothers that the children tend to go astray." Sanathana Sarathi June 1993, p. 147

But it is not just the mother's duty, the father is equally important. Swami said, *"Parents today get up from their beds quarreling with each other. When the parents wake up hurling abuses at each other, the children wake up leveling blows at each other. As is the seed, so is the plant.*

Parents today should ponder over the sacred ideas cherished by parents in the olden days. For all the bad ways followed by youth today, for all their wayward behavior and bad conduct, the parents are to blame. If the mothers are good, there will be no room for bad behavior by the children. Although parents may appear innocuous like fig fruits, they are responsible for the misbehavior of their children, like the worms inside the fruits." Sanathana Sarathi June 1993, p. 142

Our children are born as a little light into the world. As they grow and develop the light can become brighter or it can be snuffed out. We all admire a child that is polite, caring, considerate, intelligent, and of good conscience. A child that has temper tantrums, arguing, curses or talks smart, will not share his toys, belongings, or give to others is unacceptable in his behavior to most people.

If we want our children to become thoughtful and caring for us and the world, we need to give them this type of role model so that they can become what they see. But instead the children are watching TV and they are following the behavior they see on the TV. The only way we can stop this kind of behavior is by preventing our children from viewing it. We enjoy goodness in people and yet the goodness must be seen by children or else they will not know of it. We as parents can be their best and first example but they must see other role models as well. This is why Sai Baba stresses that our children should only associate with good people.

> *He said, "Talk no Evil; talk what is good.*
> *Think no Evil; think what is good.*
> *Do no Evil; do what is good.*

280

"Nature gets good or bad according to your association. Good company; Good behavior. Give no scope to bad things and get away from bad company. Always inquire who is good and who is bad?" Kodaikanal April 6, 1992

Family "sitcoms," meaning situation comedy, are presently very popular in the U.S. They depict the American family lifestyle, as it is in our present time. The greatest difficulty is that the American family lifestyle is at an all time low, and for the sake of entertainment they are more interested in making the audience laugh, instead of correcting the behavior. It is good to laugh at oneself but children need Sai values to replace the troublesome role models of screaming, put-downs, cheating, disrespect for parents etc.

The laws of nature are fixed. After a certain action there is a reaction. For example: if you as an adult watch the evening news and see starving children in the world while the international community is silent to their need, you can become angry, resentful, and helpless. Now because of what you saw you have a certain feeling and can project negative thoughts. You as an aware adult can instead project light and love to the starving people so it will take the negative feelings and transform them into positive. But how many adults have the awareness to do this? So what becomes of our children when they watch a sitcom of a typical American family stressing the behavior that is present in our culture now?

We may watch the program as a family and laugh at the child who is acting contrary to the wishes of his/her parents, e.g. throwing objects at each other, having a party and friends over with no parents at home, weird gossip about friends, yelling and screaming at each other, etc.

Our children watch other children being home alone and soon wonder why they cannot be home alone? They watch teen age parties without adult supervision and they think they are old enough. Younger children start throwing objects, smashing other children's blocks, hitting each other because they have seen it on the screen and think nothing is wrong etc.

Baba tells us, *"Because all things are available, one should not use them as he likes for the simple reason that each use is accompanied by its natural consequences. One cannot avoid these consequences. If you are prepared to face the consequences, you can act as you want. What is happening, however, is enjoyment of something with relish and later bemoaning the adverse after-effects. This is a mark of mental weakness."* Sanathana Sarathi, July 1992, p. 162

As Baba said, we enjoy pleasures but rarely do we want the consequences. Let's take the topic of fashion. I like to dress fashionably and have always enjoyed looking at the current trend. But, I am dismayed when I see my grandchildren so conscious of **labels,** without any concern of price and believing that if they do not have the right labeled clothing they will not be accepted. What about the dreaded reverse of this concept: "Will they accept others who do not dress as they do?" What kind of statement are we making when we dress? Is commercial preference enlarging the canyon of prejudice?

One evening in Swami's home, the principal of Anantapur College gave a talk. One of the things she commented on was the importance of modesty in dress for her students. She told us that people behave according to their style of dress. She said her students when dressed in white, will be reminded of purity and simplicity. When these same students are dressed in Western clothes, their behavior will tend to be more Western. She said that clothes can have an influence on our personality. I have observed my grandchildren who have developed under the dominance of "Media Overload". They are the ultimate in consumerism. They watch TV and want what they see. Every new toy or fad that comes across the screen, they know about and want to purchase it.

My oldest granddaughter who is 16 has experienced the energizing and stimulating creations of this technological age. When she was 5, she could play games on a computer. She is a whiz at "Nintendo", a high speed aggressive action game.

Because she is used to being amused by highly sophisticated entertainment; she gets "bored" very easily. We can take her to a swim park, out to eat, shopping and when she gets home she says, "I'm Bored!" After three days at Disney World, she was bored. I couldn't believe her words!!! The restlessness that we as adults experience is on the increase in the younger generations.

Swami said, *"Desires create in us restlessness. The whole world is restless. Our desires should have limits but today, desires are growing like ant hills, no limits. Desires imprison our whole life."* Kodaikanal April 4, 1992

Somehow we have been sold a "bill of goods," or convinced that a child can only grow from outside animation. From the day that a child is born in our culture they are entertained by crib toys. It seems that the world is against us getting comfortable with our own inner being.

I think we have gone to the extreme. The toy manufacturers have enticed us with glorious inventions that catch our fancy and pocketbooks. How can we reverse this pattern? How can we bring about a balance between the inner and outer world? How can we help our children to get comfortable with silence, their own thoughts, and creative play with only their own imagination.

As a child, my parents never entertained me, I would play by myself for hours getting lost in my own imagination. I would play hospital, school, house, theater, mystery. I would play the various roles in each setting. I still remember the fun, joy and satisfaction I had in these magical hours of self indulgence.

How can we teach our children that "Happiness and Peace come from within" when all they have experienced is outside pleasure from "things?" How temporary is the pleasure they derive from these material possessions or trips of entertainment, as expressed with their statements of boredom? It makes me think that we are misusing our time, energy and money.

Sai says, *"All conversations on earth is on the pleasures of earth. The time you spend for these things. If you spend the time on the Lotus Feet of the Lord, you will be saved from the gates of Hell and God will be your Savior."* Easter Sunday Discourse, April 19, 1992

The students were kept busy with a full daily schedule of activities. Swami believes that if His students are kept busy there will be less time for the mind to be distracted. They had prayers, bhajans, darshan, talks with and about Swami, field trips, nightly stories of saints and sages, and they also had chores.

Baba said, *"These three qualities can take man to noble heights. Three Human Values = 3HV*

> *1. Love of God..... hits your heart.*
> *2. Fear of Sin..... hits your head.*
> *3. Morality in Society..... hits your hand.*

Kodaikanal April 6, 1992

Since this was their vacation, Swami spoiled them with daily outings of horseback riding, walks, boating, sight seeing, picnics, and picture taking. Swami took the students everywhere; He did not give the job to someone else. He gave selflessly. It didn't seem to make any difference how much company our Beloved Baba had on His front lawn or how many guests were in His living room. His **students** came first.

I remembered how many times I would choose talking on the phone with my friends instead of giving my children my attention. Usually when I did this the children would rebel by doing something negative to get my attention.

Swami gave love to the students through His selfless actions. He never wanted anything for Himself, even though it was His Holiday! I'd have been yelping, especially after one month. He constantly attended to the needs of these students.

The amount of time that He gave to the students surprised me. He was the shepherd; they His flock. Never the two parted. These students were college and MBA's, where supervision is not nearly as critical as the age of 0 to 5 years. And yet, Baba kept them by His side for a very intense course on living with God and His principles. He was teaching us through His example that what goes in, comes out....regardless of age.

In Kodai, Swami spoke to the students about their relationship with their mother and father.

He spoke about fathers.

"Fathers are not happy when a child is born. Fathers want their children to earn a good name for the family. To uphold dharma, have humility, obedience, and discrimination. This makes Fathers happy.... not the birth."

He also spoke about the mothers.

"Students must realize that the mother is greater than God because she sacrificed her life and gave her body for their birth. If you cannot love and give to your mother what she wants or likes, how can you ever love a formless God?"

286

He described the character of children today.

"Children have no respect for parents. They are selfish, selfish, selfish. Ask your child: Where from did you come? How could you even exist if it were not for your parents? The children today think I..I..I. They have no fear of sin, no morality, no compassion, no gratitude."

In youth we lose the purity of our mind.

"Men must understand the nature of the mind. It is pure, but because of our youth; we make it dirty. We enjoy physical ornaments, we decorate ourselves, indulge in self-pleasure, and this makes the mind dirty.

Swami explained attachments to family.

"When you are a child your mother and father come first. Then you have a friend. Friend is first, parents less. Then you come to Swami and ask for a wife. Wife is first, friends less. Then you have children, wife less, children more important. Next you spend so much time thinking of work, power, fame and prosperity, children less. Soon it is time to die, and when did you have time to think of God? Can't you spend a small fraction of time thinking of God?"

Because of Mrs. Hislop's health, we were both privileged to enter Swami's house before afternoon darshan. This gave us a wonderful opportunity to have afternoon tea with Swami, plus hear and observe Sai with the students. One day in Swami's house, He praised and paid the highest respect to parents. It was a moment I will never forget.

A student asked, "Swami, are there any serious Yogis

in the Himalayan Mountains?"

Sai answered, *"Yes there are some."*

The questioner continued, "Are there any in the rest of the world?"

"Yes," said Swami. *"But Householders are my **Real Sadhakas**. They do much better! They even arise early and meditate in the morning."*

In this age of materialism, change and declining values the job of being a parent is sometimes frustrating, stressful, thankless, and overwhelming. We wonder if what we say about Sai and His teachings is ever being heard, or if our example of sacrifice is being seen and understood by our children. The children may not be listening, **but God is!** He knows the effort we make and the obstacles to overcome.

We had wonderful darshan and great satsang. The days seemed to fly away. Craig had asked Swami for an interview, and Baba replied that He would give. But as the days ticked by there was no interview. And suddenly it was time for them to depart.

It was their last darshan and Swami had not seen them yet. My desire to be with them had been fulfilled by Swami allowing me to hold the child and receive His Blessing on the first day. Since Craig and Patricia took turns coming into Swami's house, I had the grace to be with them and Swami, similar to an interview, so I was completely free to accept Swami's decision.

We were all praying to melt His Heart....

Swami approached Robert in the darshan line, "Family interview?" asked Robert. Swami remained silent. Craig sitting next to his father said, "Please, Swami?" Baba told the man next to Craig, "Go!" Swami continued walking. Craig repeated, "Please, Swami, last darshan." By now Swami was five feet away, but He turned around, looked at Craig and said, *You and wife only!"*

Craig did not hesitate, he was out of his seat instantly. When he walked across Sai's driveway, Craig raised one finger, indicating only Patricia.

When Swami opened the interview door I could hear Christian saying, "Baba, Baba, Baba." He knew Swami from the pictures on their altar. In their private interview, Baba made Christian vibhuthi and put it on his forehead and in his mouth. Baba cut his hair, signed his "Om" board and permitted Christian to take Padnamaskar. All of this Grace and only one year old.

That morning it was a joyous, good-by to Craig and family and a welcome to our son-in-law Carl, who just arrived for his first visit to see Baba. None of this was pre-arranged. Swami surprised us again.

Carl moved into Craigs room. During lunch, we talked about his first darshan with Baba, and he told us about his trip to India. The countless times Swami came to his aid by bringing the right people at just the right moment to help him. He could feel Swami's Presence with him.

Finally the time to leave Kodai was upon us. The month of April had elapsed, the sojourn with Dearest Baba was ending. There are no words to express the

Selfless Love, I observed and experienced during this month being with Baba. Plus the wealth of knowledge I had gained through so many discourses and satsangs with Sai Baba and the Hislops.

We may loose our family, friends, or possessions, but one thing is permanent forever, never to be taken from us in this life or beyond, and that is THE LOVE OF SRI SATHYA SAI BABA.

Swami said, *"One can be near to the Lord, but not dear to Him One can be far from the Lord and be dear to Him The best is to be **NEAR AND DEAR** to Him."*

The last night at Kodaikanal reminded me of the night at Brindavan when the students had to return home. Who in their right mind would want to leave Paradise with God. Saying good-bye to Swami that evening was sad.

The students sang a song after Sai Baba's discourse called "Oh Sai Maa". The emotions that were expressed by the students in song, brought tears to everyone's eyes. Some of the boys near Swami wiped the tears from their eyes, Swami gently slapped a couple of boys on the shoulder and said, *"Don't cry!"* But then I saw Swami take His handkerchief and wipe the corners of His own eyes.

"OH SAI MAA"

Oh Mother, Oh Mother, Oh Mother, Sai Mother.
You are so good, You are so innocent, so lovely are you!

Oh Mother, Oh Mother, Oh Mother, Sai Mother.

This world is a forest of thorns, while you are a
charming bed of flowers.

Oh Mother, Oh Mother, Oh Mother, Sai Mother.

Your eyes have started aching,
As You have kept awake for me through the nights.
You have sacrificed even Your sleep, to see me
peacefully sleep.

Oh Mother, Oh Mother, Oh Mother, Sai Mother.

You have no joy or sorrow of your own.
You have smiled whenever You have seen me smiling
and my crying has made you weep.
For my smiles, for my crying, You have sacrificed
Yourself.

Oh Mother, Oh Mother, Oh Mother, Sai Mother.

Mother is the very life of children.
How fortunate are all those who have a mother!
You are so beautiful, You are so cooling, ever fresh
are you.

Oh Mother, Oh Mother, Oh Mother, Sai Mother.

BHAGAVAN SRI SATHYA SAI BABA

No matter where you go, always do your duty as you see it, and know that I will be there inside you, guiding you every step of the way. In the years to come, you will experience me in many different manifestations of my form. You are my very own, dearer than dear to me. I will protect you like the eyelid protects the eye. You already have me, and I have you. I will never leave you, and you can never leave me. From this point on, do not hanker after anything. Do your duty with unwavering love, seeing all as God. Be patient; in time everything will be given to you. Be happy; there is no need to worry about anything. Whatever is experienced, whatever happens, know that this Avatar, through His Divine Will, has made it so. There is no force on earth which can delay the mission for which this Avatar has come, by even one instant. You are all sacred souls, and all have parts to play in the unfolding drama of the Golden Age, which is sure to come."

Baba's message at the end of Summer Course in Ooty, 1976.

292

DEAR TO THE LORD

"That devotee of mine, who expecting nothing, is pure, dexterous, unconcerned, free from distress and renounces all undertaking, is dear to Me."

Anapekshah Suchir-daksha Udaasino gathavyathah Sarvaarambha Parithyaagi Yomadbhakah sa me priyah. Sloka twelfth canto - Bhagavad Gita

DIVINE DISCOURSE

*T*he first quality figuring in this sloka is "Anapeksha". This term means, "to be free from any kind of expectation or desire." Can a man having a body, mind and intellect be free from desires at all? It is impossible. But such a state can be realized by an effort of will.

There are many in the world who seek sensuous pleasures from moment to moment. Most people crave for such pleasures. This method is described in the Gita as the "Preyo-maarga" (the pleasure seeking path). As against this, there is another path, which confers the experience of Self-realization and which transcends the senses. This is called the superior Righteous Path ("Sreyomaarga"). This path is not easily intelligible to all. It is not also accessible to all. Consequently, the general mass does not favor this path.

In the world, there is on the one side the attraction of the

293

"Preyo-Maarga" and on the other, the call of the "Sreyo-Maarga." However, those who seek the pleasures of the senses take to the "Preyo-Maarga". Only the Jnanis (the spiritually wise persons), who are indifferent to the fleeting mundane pleasures derived from the senses, and who are austere and pure-hearted, pursue the "Sreyo-Maarga."

There is another path, which transcends the path of "Preyas" (pleasure) and "Sreyas" (virtue). These two paths encompass all the possible desires of human beings. "Anapeksha" goes beyond both of them. "Anapeksha" is described as "being free from desires." But this is not wholly correct. It is when a man gives up the feeling, in the performance of all actions, that "I am the doer" (the sense of ego), "I am the experiencer" (the sense of fulfillment of desire), that true "Anapeksha" emerges. This means that conceit of doership and the sense of enjoyment of desired things should be wholly renounced. This is the true state of desirelessness "Anapeksha." It is only when all actions are done as an offering to God that "Anapeksha" prevails. When such a feeling fills the heart of the devotee, the Divine confers beatitude on him. Such a devotee is dear to the Lord. If you want to earn the love of the Lord, you have to render service to anyone, anywhere, as an offering to the Lord.

The second quality is "Suchi" (Purity). There should be both inner and outer purity. Bodily purity relates to the physical. It covers such cleansing acts as bathing, wearing clean clothes, eating pure food and the like. Even in studies, the books should be wholesome and elevating. But mere external cleanliness without internal purity is of no value.

Everyone, from the scholar to the common man, is concerned only about external cleanliness and not about the purity of the heart within. However pure the ingredients may be, if the vessel in which they are cooked is not clean, the food will be spoiled. For a man, his heart is the vessel, and he must see that it is kept pure and untainted. For the purification of the heart, everyone must undertake selfless service. Attachments and aversions, which pollute the mind, should be eschewed by concentrating on Seva. It is only when the heart is pure that selfless service can be performed. Hence, both bodily and mental purity are essential for a good devotee.

The third quality is "Daksha". This means that everyone should regard his life as a form of penance. Everyone must have a firm resolution ("Daksha") that as long as life lasts he will dedicate himself to the service of his fellowmen. Thereby he will realize his oneness with all mankind. Such a feeling of unity will lead to God-Realization. Service is the only way to get rid of selfishness and self-centeredness. A devotee who has resolved upon such service is dear to the Lord.

The fourth quality is "Udaaseenah." This means indifference towards sorrow and joy, loss or gain, honor or dishonor. You must be concerned only to see whether your actions are pure and selfless according to your conscience. Nothing else matters, neither the praise nor the blame of other people. When your conscience tells you that what you are doing is good, you may go ahead regardless of the opinions of others, whether they are your kinsmen, friends or others. This is the true meaning of "Udaaseenah" (indifference). You should not be swayed by fears or threats. In this context, it is advisable for devotees to keep away from politics. Sometimes, out of a desire for recognition or publicity, one may be tempted to cultivate men in power. This temptation corrupts your mind. By developing the spirit of indifference in its best sense, you must seek to serve all with a feeling of love. "Indifference" should not assume the form of arrogance or ostentatious condescension. Adhere to what is right and turn away from what is bad. That is the highest "Udaaseenatha."

The next quality is "Gathavyathah" (free from worry). This means that there should be no worry regarding what is past. A man with worries can never accomplish anything. One should not worry about what is past or what is in the womb of the future. It is such worry that is the cause of all of man's troubles. There is no meaning in worrying about the unknown future. Keeping the present in view, men should engage themselves in right actions. The past and the future are in the present. Devotees who do their duty in the present are dear to the Lord.

The sixth quality is "Sarvaarambha Parithyaagi" (renunciation of all undertakings). This means that there should be no ostentation or showing off in any undertaking by a devotee. Unless ostentation is given up, egoism will not go. The ego must be eliminated for purifying the heart. No good deed can be done without purity in the heart. It is through sacred deeds that the heart is purified. Ostentation is a demonic quality. It encourages egoism and megalomania. One should seek to acquire a good name through selfless service alone. It should be done with humility and sincerity. One who aspires to become a national leader must first know how to render service. He should not seek office or position. The Sai organizations have been set up for rendering service and not to establish official positions. Seva should be done out of a sense of duty.

Seva brings out all that is great in man. It broadens the heart and widens one's vision. It fills one with joy. It promotes unity. It proclaims the truth of the Spirit. It drives out all the evil qualities in a man. It must be regarded as a great spiritual discipline. You are born to serve, not to dominate. Everyone in the world is a servant and not a master. All relationships, of husband and wife, mother and child, the employer and employee, are based on mutual service. The world is progressing because of such mutual service. If the principle of service did not operate, the world would come to a halt. Do you regard an "officer" as a superior? It is not so. Even he is a servant. It is only when man is filled with the spirit of service that his divine nature is revealed. He then experiences the peace that passeth understanding.

What is the reason for the lack of peace in the world today? It is because there is no harmony in thought, word, and deed in the lives of the people. Peace must begin in the family, in the home. When there is understanding and harmony in the family, peace will spread to the community and from there to the nation and the world. Hence, unity is the primary need today. Unity confers joy and peace.

Transformation must begin with the individual. When

the individual changes, the world will change. This transformation has to take place in the minds of men. Right thoughts will lead to right actions. That is why the scriptures have declared that the mind is the cause of man's bondage or liberation.

Fifth World Conference
November 20, 1990
Sanathana Sarathi
January 1991 p. 1